# YOU DON'T NEED ANYONE'S PERMISSION

## TO LIVE YOUR BEST LIFE!

A Real Talk Journey
to Living Your Authentic Life

DONNA SCOATES-NIXON

Copyright © 2021 The Lazy Man's Way to Riches, LLC

All rights reserved. No part of this publication may be reproduced, distributed, or transmitted in any form or by any means, including photocopying, recording, or other electronic or mechanical methods, without the prior written permission of the author. For permission requests, email the publisher at www.youdontneedanyonespermission.com

Ordering Information: Donnanixon@youdontneedanyonespermission.com

Special discounts are available on quantity purchases by corporations, associations, and others. For details, contact the publisher at the email above.

Cover and interior design AnnetteWoodGraphics.com

Printed in the United States of America.

Library of Congress Control Number: 2021911248

ISBN 978-1-884337-04-8

"To *Have* More...One Must First *Become* More."

Joe Karbo

This book is dedicated to

Joe Karbo who had a quest to become more,

My love Richard who helped me become more,

My Partner, Best Friend and Life Coach Donna Quarles
who consistently supports me becoming more,

My dear friend Stephen who believed in me
and supported me having more,

And my family who never made me feel
I needed permission to "do me" or want more!

#blessedbythemall

# CONTENTS

## BUILDING THE FOUNDATION OF CHANGE

| | | |
|---|---|---|
| INTRO | AN INTENTIONAL SHIFT TO YOUR BEST LIFE! | 1 |
| CHAPTER 1 | WHAT TO EXPECT | 7 |
| CHAPTER 2 | DO YOU HAVE WHAT IT TAKES? | 13 |
| CHAPTER 3 | NOW, TELL ME WHAT YOU WANT... WHAT YOU REALLY REALLY WANT! | 23 |
| CHAPTER 4 | BELIEF AND A BURNING DESIRE | 33 |
| CHAPTER 5 | THE SWEET SPOT | 41 |
| CHAPTER 6 | BURNING DESIRES INTO GOALS | 55 |
| CHAPTER 7 | TOP 10 LIST TO TURN YOUR GOALS INTO REALITY | 63 |

## TOOLS FOR CHANGE

| | | |
|---|---|---|
| CHAPTER 8 | IT'S THE LAW! | 73 |
| CHAPTER 9 | THE ULTIMATE MINDHACK | 77 |
| CHAPTER 10 | I DECLARE | 89 |
| CHAPTER 11 | A SUPER SUGGESTION | 97 |

## WHAT'S THE HOLD UP

| CHAPTER 12 | WHO'S THE BOSS? | 103 |
| CHAPTER 13 | BE THE CHANGE | 111 |
| CHAPTER 14 | YOU'VE BEEN HYPNOTIZED | 121 |
| CHAPTER 15 | OH WHERE, OH WHERE, DID MY SELF-ESTEEM GO? | 129 |
| CHAPTER 16 | THE DAILY MIND F**K | 137 |
| CHAPTER 17 | YOU'VE GOT SOME UNPACKING TO DO | 145 |
| CHAPTER 18 | BYE FELICIA! | 159 |
| CHAPTER 19 | THE TRICKLE-DOWN EFFECT | 167 |
| CHAPTER 20 | HABITS; THE GOOD, THE BAD, & THE UGLY | 175 |

## NEXT LEVEL LIVING

| CHAPTER 21 | TURNING POINTS, DECISIONS AND A LIFE FULL OF SOMEDAY'S | 185 |
| CHAPTER 22 | BE GRATEFUL, BE KIND AND BE A BLESSING | 193 |
| CHAPTER 23 | WHAT'S NEXT? | 197 |

# AN INTENTIONAL SHIFT TO YOUR BEST LIFE!

*"There is only one success…to be able to live your life in your own way."*

Christopher Morley

Welcome to the first day of your Best Life. There's a good chance you chose this book because you're feeling stuck in one or more areas of your life. The good news is you don't have to stay there. You're grown! **You don't need anyone's permission** to take time for yourself and decide what you want and need to get unstuck and move your life forward. This is your life after all.

Maybe one of the reasons you're stuck is because it's easy to lose sight of that when your life is full of taking care of everyone else's needs or just getting the bills paid. I recently read an article about a woman who was "grieving herself." She had lost herself catering to everyone else and was grieving her former happy self with hopes and dreams. Now her hope was just to get 10 minutes to herself. Sound familiar?

With that said, it's important to point out as we start this journey together, that it's *your* definition of your Best Life that matters here. This is all about you. Not your spouse, or kids, parents, or boss. Now is the time for you to set your current life down for a few weeks and focus on you, the true expression of you…the authentic you and the life you want so you don't end up grieving yourself.

> **The late Steve Jobs of Apple famously said;**
>
> *"Your time is limited, so don't waste it living someone else's life.*
>
> *Don't be trapped by Dogma, which is living with the results of other people's thinking.*
>
> *Don't let the noise of other's opinions drown out your own inner voice.*
>
> *And most important, have the courage to follow your heart and intuition."*

Those are words to live by… and with what you'll learn in the pages of this book, I'm going to help you live them.

## True Story

This book is based on a true story. Yes, I said story because it was born back in the day from the journey of a man named Joe Karbo who went from being broke to becoming a multimillionaire. When he was broke and had 8 children to feed, he realized that what he was doing wasn't working. It became clear to him that he was going to have to make some changes in his life to become successful. He later stated it as…To *have* more, he was going to have to first *become* more.

> **THOSE ARE WORDS TO LIVE BY...
> AND WITH THIS BOOK I'M GOING
> TO HELP YOU LIVE THEM.**

What does that mean? It means that all the things he had learned and done to that point got him to where he was, but it wasn't getting him any further. He was just getting by. He was tired of the drama. Tired of worrying about how he was going to feed everyone and pay the bills. He wanted to be successful and he wanted his freedom. Freedom to do what he wanted, when, how and where he wanted. No limitations. We can all relate to that, right?

So, he got to work on making the intentional shift to *become more*; focusing on getting rid of those things in his life that weren't working for him and enhancing those things that made him a better human. Slowly and steadily it worked in both his personal and business life. He became happier and rich and got the freedom he was looking for.

He then wanted others to learn what he had learned, so he wrote a book; *The Lazy Man's Way to Riches,* that chronicled his story about his journey to *his riches*...his Best Life.

He devoted the last years of his life to making sure others were given the tools to *become more* as he had done by teaching the personal growth principles of his original journey to success. That book has sold millions of copies, been the subject of many high-profile newspaper and magazine articles through the years, has changed the lives of those who practiced what they learned from it and *is the genesis of this literary legacy.*

My late husband Richard G. Nixon (yes, his real name) was an incredibly successful businessman who retired early and was living the life. He was chillin' on his boat in Rio but eventually realized he was unfulfilled because he had no purpose. That's when he had an idea that changed the course of his life. He had been a student of Joe's book and attributed much of his success to the power principles he learned from it. He decided he wanted to carry on Joe's mission. He too wanted others to learn what he had learned, to be able to live their best life.

So, he bought the company and dedicated himself to revising and updating it for a new generation. I came into the picture at that point and we worked on it together, self-publishing it before it then went on to be published by two major publishers and promoted globally. All these years later, the literary legacy still lives on, has become an international success and been translated into eight languages so far because it has helped millions around the world find their success and best life.

**YOU'LL LEARN TO BE UN-COMMON AND THINK LIKE SOME OF THE MOST SUCCESSFUL PEOPLE ON THE PLANET.**

I now have the honor of making it my mission to continue the legacy of Joe Karbo, and continue with the vision Richard and I had for this powerful life changing book by bringing it to new generations around the world with technology neither of them could've imagined. You'll learn more about me throughout, but the main thing to know is my life has been dedicated to this for over 25 years. I've written it, I've lived it and I've taught it so you're getting years of experience from all three of us.

I wanted to give you that background story, so you know that the legacy this book is based on has been internationally successful for decades because the core principles are timeless and for everyone. Meaning, no matter what the year is, where you live, how old you are and how much or how little you have in your life…the core principles will always be relevant.

So, with that said, you'll hear me reference Joe and Richard periodically, and some of their words are woven throughout mine. However…I've added my own vision, given it a way more "PC" title and revised and updated it for today's world with current references, wisdom learned and new insights that have evolved since Joe and Richard's day.

## Now Back To You

Those core principles are what you'll use to re-build your foundation so you can get everything you want out of your life from this point forward.

Yes, I said everything. It's common for people to think there's a limit to what you can be, do and have. You'll soon realize that you're the one who put those limits there, so you're the one with the power to remove them. I'll go into more detail later but suffice it to say that no matter what the definition of your best life is, this book teaches you how to get there.

You'll gain the tools to remove those limiting beliefs and learn other secrets to finally give you the permanent change you've been wanting. You'll learn to be *un*-common and think like some of the most successful people on our planet.

So lean in. As Steve Jobs said, have the courage to follow your heart and intuition. Let me guide you through the changes as you make the Intentional Shift to be able to live your life in your own way. 100%! Your best life.

**Let the intentional shifting begin!**

# WHAT TO EXPECT

*"Drop anything that weighs you down.
Protect & nourish all the things in life that uplift you."*

Gurumayi Chidvilasananda

Have you ever been asked a question that made you think and shifted your point of view? That's what we're going to be doing here. I'll be asking some of the questions you may not have ever asked yourself, to make you think and help shift your point of view if the current view has you stuck. Oprah Winfrey calls it Big Picture Pondering. I like that description for what we'll do together, because there's nothing bigger than the rest of your life.

Now is the time for a refresh. Since Covid-19 came into our lives, the life we were living was put on an involuntary pause and we all did some unexpected shifting because of it. You've probably had to ask yourself some questions you never intended to ask about your job, your relationships and where you spend your time and energy. It's brought out some ugly truths about the lives and relationships of some people and strengthened the positive truths of others. You may have discovered that people you gave your heart and soul, or blood sweat and tears to, whether personal or professional, just weren't that into you when the going got tough.

We've all been given a reality check of how precious time is and what we do with that time. We've rediscovered the value of family and friends that showed us they'll be there for us when everything is stripped from life as we know it. It's brought clarity to the things we may have taken for granted previous to the pandemic and put a higher value on freedom since we've been deprived of it in certain ways during this pandemic.

With the life refresh you'll get by reading this book, comes those big picture questions that bring awareness to the good things we want to protect and nourish, as well as the habits and people that drag us down and need released. So now is the time to use this pause in our normal daily life to your advantage. Now is the time for you to have what you really want because as we've all been reminded, the cliché saying, "Life's too short," is painfully true.

## Shifting

So, I talked in the Intro about shifting. Let me explain that a bit more. Shifting has become a buzz word for something people have been doing forever…changing…moving from one position or direction to another. In this case, to a better position.

Below is something I found on the internet that explains Intentional Shifting perfectly. There was no name attached to it or I would've given credit where credit is due, but I wanted to include it here because of not only the great explanation of the term, but it also explains what you can expect from reading this…intentionally.

> **"As you are shifting, you will begin to realize that you are not the same person you used to be.**
>
> **The things you used to tolerate have become intolerable.**

> When you once remained quiet, you are now speaking your truth.
>
> When you once battled and argued, you are now choosing to remain silent.
>
> You are beginning to understand the value of your voice and there are some situations that no longer deserve your time, energy and focus."

That's it in a nutshell. You can expect to make some changes, find your voice and most importantly, speak your truth. You can expect to drop the things that are weighing you down and learn to nourish all the things in life that uplift you. You can expect to make some shifts for the better. You deserve it. You have the right to be happy. You have the right to be successful. You have the right to be who you want to be. You have the right to "Do you."

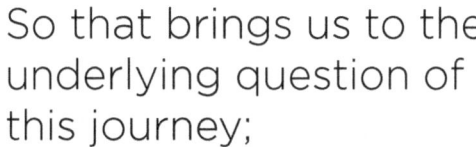

So that brings us to the underlying question of this journey;
## What does it mean to "do you?"

I'll walk you through the process of discovering your answers to that question and a few more of the most fundamental questions in your life such as;

- Who are you at this point in your life?

- Are you who you want to be… or have you become someone else's version of you?

- Are you living the life you want to be living?

- Are you living your purpose?
  Do you even know what your purpose is?

- **Do you know what you want?**

- **Do you have a plan to get there or are you just *getting through* life?**

They look like easy questions. No-brainers, right? Of course, you know who you are and what you want. But as we break these basics down into more detail and go through the several layers of these questions, you may find it requires a little more thought and angst than you were expecting.

You'll evaluate and break your life down, to be able to build it back stronger. I understand if that gets you nervous, but I hope it also gets you excited because if you take time to evaluate where you are and what you really want for your life, nothing will be able to stop you from getting it after learning the principles of change you'll find here.

About now you might be thinking, Yikes, what did I get myself into? I know it's a lot. Take a deep breath and let's continue…

# Growth

Growth happens when there is a shift, so you will definitely grow during this journey. It happens in three different ways.

First, growth by starting something new. As you read through this, you'll be motivated and challenged to make new decisions. You get to do new things and try new approaches. One reader described it as an evolution happening in his head. It's your choice. You're in control of you and what happens next. That in itself might feel like a new concept.

Second, growth doesn't have to mean *doing* something. It can come by *stopping* something you're doing that isn't working for you or is getting in the way of a better you.

Richard used to say, "If you just keep doing what you're doing, you'll just keep getting what you're getting."

> YOU CAN EXPECT A PATH TO HEALING...AS YOU BECOME MORE AWARE AND TAKE CONTROL BACK.

Right? You need to stop doing those things or you won't ever move onward and upward in your life. I know, easy for me to say. I realize that some of those things you're doing are going to be tough to stop, but you're going to learn the principles to stop putting roadblocks in your own way as we go through this journey together.

Third, growth comes through the mistakes we've made. Mistakes are a part of life. They can easily turn into excuses for why you aren't moving forward, but if you learn from them and make corrections, they become steppingstones to your better life.

## And Healing

You can expect a path to healing from some of the things in your past...a healing of your spirit from where you've been and what you've gone through so far in your life, as we talk through some of your experiences with some real talk. You'll become more aware, take control back, and make those experiences steppingstones to your best life.

To sum it up, this will take you on a journey...a place where you think, learn, heal, and grow. You'll learn what it is to "do you" for maybe the first time in your life. You'll become more confident and capable, which will not only make you feel better but will help you make the right choices and changes as you move forward to the best you.

Aren't you excited to get started? I'm excited for you because it's so liberating and empowering to do you… the authentic you. So, let's get to it. Now that I've gone through what I'll provide to help you succeed on this journey, let's talk about what you'll need to be successful going to the next level.

# DO YOU HAVE WHAT IT TAKES?

*"One of the most courageous things you can do is identify yourself, know who you are, what you believe in, and where you want to go."*

Sheila Murray Bethel

## What do you need for a successful journey to your Best Life?

Before I answer that, let me mention a few things you DON'T need, because those are the self-limiting roadblocks that stop most people before they even get started. Let me do the heavy lifting and remove these for you so you can move forward without hesitation.

 ## The first one you don't need is a college degree.

Many people think a college degree is essential for success, and some even think it should be from a particular school. Not true. Though I'm a big proponent of higher education, a college degree doesn't guarantee success, and a lack of a degree doesn't guarantee you won't be successful. Plain and simple.

To prove my point, here are a few business people you may have heard of that didn't let a lack of a college degree get in the way of their success;

- **Mark Zuckerberg**
  One of the most recognized names in tech. Started Facebook. He dropped out of Harvard during his sophomore year to work on FB full time. He's now worth Billions. Successful…Yep!

- **Steve Jobs**
  Co-founder of Apple and Pixar dropped out of college after just 6 months to start Apple. Was he successful? Uh, yeah.

- **Bill Gates**
  Co-founder of Microsoft. He dropped out of Harvard to focus on building his company. I think one of the richest men in the world proved a college degree isn't necessary to success! I could add to the list for days, but you get the idea.

## The second thing you don't need is money.

Speaking of business, maybe you're one of those who thinks it takes money to make money. Yes, I realize having money helps but it's not a deal breaker. Do a google search and you'll find all sorts of successful people that started with nothing and still hit crazy success. Here's just a few to prove the point.

- **Jan Koum who invented "Whatsapp"** was born into poverty in the Ukraine. He focused on learning computers and after emigrating to the U.S., he worked for Yahoo where he got the idea for Whatsapp. He's no longer poor in case you were wondering. Facebook bought the app for billions.

- **Steve Jobs and Steve Woznizk of Apple.** Again, Steve as an example. After he dropped out of college, well you know the famous story…they started developing early models of the first Apple computer in his parents' garage. They had to find someone else to sign on as a guarantee to get the bank loan to start the business. His legacy is everywhere we look nowadays. Chances are you're reading this book on a newer generation of something that was created in his garage back in the day.

- **Oprah Winfrey; The poster child for success.** This global icon was born into poverty in rural Mississippi and raised in the inner city of Milwaukee. Not the steppingstones you would expect for iconic success. She worked her way up through the radio and TV industry to become a millionaire by the age of 32.

Guess I can stop here. Point made. Oprah had not only poverty against her but other roadblocks that could have left her playing victim for the rest of her life. She's a bad ass that didn't let anything stop her.

## The third thing you don't need is youth.

How many people do you know who think their best is behind them? People of any age who think they've missed the best of their life and now feel it's too late, so they've given up and are content just *getting through* life instead of *living* life.

Well, whether you're in your 30's or 80's…**it's never too late**. There are many people who didn't even get started on the path to success until later in life, and some people decide to switch gears and do something completely different later in life. Actress Patricia Heaton, best known for her role in the TV show "Everybody Loves Raymond," wrote a book about reinventing yourself as you get older, entitled *Your Second Act*. At 47, actress Traci Ellis Ross known for the TV show "Blackish" and already living the life of success, decided to embrace her second act, and completely switch her lane by embracing her talent as a singer in the film "High Note." Who knew she could sing? She said in a recent interview that she feels it's never too late to change your lane. That's what I'm saying.

There are of course many others, even fictional characters. I saw this beautiful movie on Netflix called "Edie" about an 83-year-old woman who decides it's never too late to go for what she wants. After her controlling husband that kept her isolated dies, her controlling daughter wants to move her to a nursing home. As she begrudgingly visits the place, she

> WHETHER YOU'RE IN YOUR 30'S OR 80'S…
> IT'S NEVER TOO LATE.

sees all her peers sitting around just waiting to die. She goes home, leaves her daughter a message that she's leaving town and embarks on a solo trip from England to Scotland to fulfill her lifelong dream of climbing a mountain in the Scottish Highlands. Spoiler Alert: with some trouble and help, she does make it to the top.

I know it's a fictional character, but the reality of the story is valid. I know real people that have lived lives disturbingly close to hers but without the happy ending. Point is, no matter what your age it's never too late to go after your dream. The best *can be* yet to come.

## A Few Things You DO Need

Ok, now let's look at a few things you *do* need for going next level…to your best life.

 An Open Mind

The famous artist Georgia O'Keeffe once said, "I decided to start anew, to strip away what I had been taught." This book is about you being able to have everything you want. But to do that you have to be willing to strip away a lot of what you've been taught and start anew. Maybe some things you learned were wrong, maybe some things have changed. I know for a fact that *you* will change as you go through this, so keep an open mind. You bought this book for a reason. It won't do you any good if you keep a closed mind and are unwilling to make any changes.

Let me give you a personal example of how a closed mind can affect success. My late husband was friends with Mark Victor Hansen, the motivational speaker and co-author of the now mega hit book series *Chicken Soup for the Soul*. Back in the day, before it was published, Mark came to my husband and asked him what he thought of the book and would he consider publishing it. My normally brilliant husband wrote a rejection note on the original manuscript stating, "Mark, nobody is going to want to read all these sappy, bleeding heart sob stories." It kills me to this day. That was pre-me so I wasn't around to open his mind and set him straight, or I'd be a gazillionaire today. I later reminded him of this many times when I needed him to have an open mind about something. He was not amused.

As you read this, you may hear things you've heard before, but you may hear it this time in a way that gives you your "Aha" moment. Some things may sound a little more "WooWoo" than you're used to and some you may not agree with. One thing's for sure, you're going to get loaded up with a bunch of nuggets that can change your life. The degree in which they do is up to you, and how open your mind is.

##  Belief

You need to believe in yourself. Actor Will Smith said that he feels greatness is accessible to everyone, if you can *believe* it. Agreed.

The power of beliefs is life-changing either way, good or bad. Limiting beliefs can be what's been holding you back for years or possibly your whole life. This book shows you a way to transform your belief system from a passive, limiting force into a positive, dynamic force.

FYI…Along your journey others may try to push your "limiting beliefs button." They may try to disprove the theories because they want to hold you back and keep you at their level. Don't worry about the others. Do you! Those same people will soon be asking you how you changed your life so drastically because they'll want the same for themselves.

##  An Attitude Adjustment

Your thoughts create your reality and your future, so make them good. This goes along with #1 and #2 because some of you will need an Attitude Adjustment to be open to a new belief system and an open mind.

Another part of that attitude adjustment is getting rid of the excuses… the limiting beliefs… that have held you down until now. "It's too late for me now. I'm too old," or "I would have had a successful career, but I got pregnant." Or "I'm not doing what I want because my parents didn't want me to have the career I really wanted." Any of these sound familiar?

Whatever the excuse, you're not alone. Those are three I heard just this week from people in my daily life. Everyone finds ways to excuse their lack of success. I could go on and on listing all the rationalizations, justifications and excuses I've heard people give through the years for not getting all they want out of life.

The problem is with your attitudes about yourself, not your limitations. Don't put the time and energy into holding on to barriers that exist only in your mind. Put that energy into building yourself up. Give yourself an attitude adjustment and focus on the positive. It's as simple as a mind shift and only you have the power to do it.

##  Willingness To Take Action And Make Changes

Most of us are where we are now because of input fed to us as we were growing up. Input from our role models: parents, teachers, and the myriad of other people who formed and guided our lives. It seemed like the voice of God speaking to us when we were younger so we accepted the input without question, but think about it, they were just average people with their opinions. You're now old enough to have your own opinions and make your own decisions, but have chosen to stay stuck with theirs…until now.

Just because you've "done it this way your whole life" doesn't mean you need to keep doing it that way. If you truly want a better you and a better life, it's up to you to accept responsibility for erasing the crap from your past and applying the new information being offered to you.

Unfortunately, unwillingness to change is a big roadblock people put in their own way. People just don't like change; it's too uncomfortable to go out of their comfort zone. But remember as Richard used to say; "If you just keep doing what you're doing…You'll just keep getting what you're getting." Meaning to be *un*-common, and to get what you want in life, it will require some changes or everything will remain the same.

One of those changes is…You have to take action! Reading about it is definitely going to change your life, but in my experience…taking action on what you're learning and applying it to your life is the game changer. So, you'll hear me say "Write it down" throughout the book.

The poet Alice Walker once wrote that her "words traveled down her arm." So make this interactive, get a notebook and let your words "travel down your arm" as you evaluate your life. It gets you involved, holds you accountable and is a constant reinforcement of what you want.

Note: For those that want an even more interactive experience, I offer an online course based on this book, with downloadable action step exercises designed to isolate some of the most important principles from the book. And I guide you by talking you through the course, sharing my personal stories of how I've used these principles in my life. Information with an exclusive discount code for you is provided at the end of the book.

> JUST BECAUSE YOU'VE "DONE IT THIS WAY YOUR WHOLE LIFE" DOESN'T MEAN YOU NEED TO KEEP DOING IT THAT WAY.

 ## Commitment

This is the most important action you can take. The successful people I mentioned previously didn't quit. They stayed committed to their dreams, their vision of success, and the path they laid out for themselves to get there. Do that.

Remember this is for you. I know I've said it before, and you'll hear it again, because I can't tell you the number of people I've seen through the years who let someone else's wants, needs, or words get in their way of staying committed on the path to their dreams of a better life. Don't be a victim to that. Don't let someone else hold you back, and keep your world small.

And don't let yourself get in the way either. You'll be learning new things, and you'll be challenged about some of your current beliefs and attitudes. That might get you stuck or overwhelmed, but that's completely normal and understandable. That's a part of growth.

By keeping your focus and not giving up, you will achieve your best life.

## And So It Begins…

Now that you know what to expect, and what you do and don't need, let's get you started. Are you ready?

## CHAPTER 3

# NOW, TELL ME WHAT YOU WANT... WHAT YOU REALLY REALLY WANT!

*"I always wanted to be somebody, but I should've been more specific."*

Lily Tomlin

"When I was getting out of the service, this old marine major said to me, 'What do you want to do with your life?'"

"I said, 'Well, I think I want to go into television, but I don't know if I have the talent.'"

"He took his two shoes that he was shining, and he smashed them together and said, 'Don't you know you can have anything you want in this life? You've just got to want it bad enough! Now, do you really want it?'"

> *"I said, 'Yes sir, I do.' And that's when I charged out of my Enlisted Quarters, got in my Hudson convertible and went to Hollywood and began knocking on doors."*

This was from an *Esquire* magazine interview with Regis Philbin. You may recognize his name because he ended up having the talent to stay on TV for six decades, most notably with his morning talk show "Live with Regis and Kathie Lee" (and then Kelly), and as the original host of the TV game show, "Who Wants to be a Millionaire."

With a little prodding from a mentor, he admitted what he wanted which gave him the direction he needed to go get it. Because of it, Regis ended up having a 60-year career doing what he loved up until the very end of his life and becoming a multimillionaire himself.

No matter how old you are, right now I'm your mentor prodding you to admit what it is *you* want, because you're now on your way to having *everything* you really want!

Notice I say "everything," not "anything." There's an important difference!

If someone were to give you *anything* you ask for, it would automatically be *limited* because it really means any *one* thing. More would be withheld than given. Make sense?

To have *everything*, means having *no limits*! Good point, right? Why limit ourselves to just any-*one*-thing, when we can have everything?

## WHY LIMIT OURSELVES TO JUST ANY-ONE-THING, WHEN WE CAN HAVE EVERYTHING?

## No Doubt

So, let me say it again; you're now on the way to having everything in the world you want!

Now, what was your reaction when you read that sentence? Did you start to reject even the possibility of that happening? Did your habit-conditioned mind automatically say, "Not me . . . No way."

Well stop it. Don't be guilty of self-limitation. Don't reject the life you can have, by letting your limiting beliefs stop you from being open minded enough to learn how to get it. Just keep that mind open and pay attention. #whynot?

## Two Power Principles For Success

Soon you'll be asked to come up with a detailed, specific answer to the question; What do you want?

Why do you need a specific inventory of what you want? Because a clear and specific plan is one of the power principles of truly successful people, both in business and in life.

Here's a list of some of the other things that come to mind when we think of a person's success. From this list, select what you feel are the other qualities successful people have in common.

1. Luck
2. Family background
3. Social status
4. Intelligence

5. Education advantage

6. Good health

7. Enthusiasm

8. Winning personality

9. Determination

10. Plenty of money

**Take time to examine the choices carefully before you go to the next page!**

## You're wrong!

Sorry. It's a trick question. The correct answer, the other quality that all successful people have in common, wasn't even listed. Wait, what?

Doesn't the list include the things we're accustomed to thinking of when we think of success? Yes, the list does include the qualities we're told we need to succeed or have learned to believe we need to succeed in life. I bet you picked at least one from the group. But the fact is many people have had combinations of those qualities and have failed big time. And others have been successful, ones who from the beginning start off behind the 8 ball with poverty, no education, or health problems.

Now I'll tell you the 2 power principles you *do* need that *weren't* on the list;

The first power principle necessary for success in life: is to **know what you want and have a clearly defined plan written down to get it.** By articulating your wants and writing them down, you're making an announcement to yourself that you're serious and creating a roadmap to keep you on track.

The second power principle necessary for success in life: is **the ability to use effectively and confidently whatever asset you have.** In other words, start where you are, with what you have and build off of that. It isn't what you have that counts, but how effectively you use it. Steve Jobs had a garage and made the time and commitment to devote to his passion. Get it?

So now comes that big question...

**What do you want?**

What represents your best life to you?

Think about all the things that you feel would represent success to you and your life…money, work, health, material things, relationships, a balanced life. Only you know what that is. Write it down.

I remember seeing an interview with Oprah once where she explained her vision of success was trees. Yes, you heard me right, trees. Growing up, the homes in the neighborhood of prosperous people had lots of big, beautiful mature trees, so that always represented success to her. If you watch any of the shows done from her Santa Barbara home, you'll notice she does her interviews sitting in the gorgeous backyard absolutely covered with, you guessed it…big, beautiful mature trees.

...AND NOT DRIFT BACK TO THE HABIT OF LIVING SOMEONE ELSE'S IDEA OF YOU.

So, don't worry if your view of success isn't the conventional view of success from others. Don't worry about others and what they think. Ralph Waldo Emerson said "What I must do is all that concerns me. Not what people think." What's important is to know what *you* really want out of life. Again, this is about you. I'll keep saying it because I want you to stay aware of *your* needs and not drift back to the habit of living someone else's idea of you.

## A Trip To Your "Someplace"

Can you imagine a man going to the nearest airport to catch a plane with only the vaguest idea of where he wanted to go? Picture this; he goes to the counter and says he wants a ticket to "Somewhere." If you were the ticket seller, what would you do to help him?

> **Man:** I'd like a ticket, please.
>
> **You:** Certainly, sir, where to?
>
> **Man:** Oh . . . uh . . . some place nice.
>
> **You:** I don't understand.
>
> **Man:** Well, I need to "get someplace," I don't want to just waste time.
>
> **You:** Someplace like where?
>
> **Man:** Someplace where I can be happy. Where I can have a good income. Get a new car. Maybe become an executive with a good company or even have my own business. Be able to take care of my family. You know, I'd like to get someplace where things are really great for me and my family. Just give me a ticket. I'll pay for it, whatever the cost.
>
> **You:** But, sir, I can't sell you a ticket until you know exactly where you want to go.

Wouldn't that be your reaction? You'd have no way to help this guy until he could tell you where he wanted to go. Well, isn't that what you've been saying to life? Without knowing what you want and having clear, well-defined goals to get it, your destination of success and your best life is impossible.

This book is to help you discover your "Someplace." The questions I ask are on purpose to help you through the process of getting there.

Nearly 800 years ago, the Persian poet Rumi wrote "You must ask for what you really want." That's as relevant today as when he said it centuries ago.

By articulating your wants, you're making an announcement to yourself and the universe that you're serious. So, let's get serious.

Think about these three intentional questions. Write them down. Make three lists with your answers, because as we continue through the book, you'll learn the principles of change and the ultimate mind hack to help you get the things on these lists.

 Needs

What are your current Needs; The things you need taken care of ASAP to be able to breathe? Like all your credit cards paid off. Yeah..that will be on most people's list.

 Wants

What do you want…really, really want? (Sorry had to do it.) This is all the things you dream about wanting for yourself. Let yourself go to that "I wish" place in your mind.

## Personality Qualities

What Personality Qualities do you feel you're lacking in and will need to strengthen or build to be able to level up? If you have trouble, think about people you admire and respect and what qualities you feel they have that you'd like to have.

I know your needs will probably flow out no problem. But the other two lists might be a bit tougher. It's hard to focus on yourself when possibly decades have been spent caring about other's needs and wants. Trust, I've heard the struggles from others. Lots of others.

But remember…we've already talked about how this is your time to focus on you, right? So, stop thinking about everyone else's wants and needs, and finally admit what it is *you* want.

The simple act of admitting what you want and writing it down, seems to awaken a sleeping giant within you. Trust. It will start "gnawing" at you until you let it out.

# BELIEF AND A BURNING DESIRE

> *"Desire is the starting point of all achievement. Not a hope, not a wish, but a keen pulsating desire which transcends everything."*
>
> Napoleon Hill

Andrew Carnegie, as in Carnegie Hall, was an uneducated immigrant who started with nothing and built an enormous business empire. Later, as a successful businessman he was interviewed by a young talented writer named Napoleon Hill, and what was planned as a 3-hour interview turned into a 3-day interview. It ended with him commissioning Napoleon to interview other successful men to find out what they thought were the qualities of success.

Using the magic of the Carnegie name, Napoleon was able to speak to several hundred of the most successful business and political leaders of the time including Alexander Graham Bell, Thomas Edison, John D.

Rockefeller, and Woodrow Wilson. It was from these interviews that he created his now classic famous book, *Think and Grow Rich*.

During those interviews, he found thirteen universal principles that anyone could apply to become successful. Not everyone interviewed had all thirteen, but there were two assets you could use to help get the other eleven. You're going to need these two to go next level. Don't worry if you don't already have them, because you'll learn how to develop them as you read on.

## So, what are they?

## A Burning Desire

The first is a Burning Desire.

Is what you want really important to you? I mean *really* important or is it just what I call a *"wouldn't it be nice if"* desire? "Wouldn't it be nice if" I had a million dollars? or "Wouldn't it be nice if" we had a home on the beach?

Everybody has those kinds of desires, but they seem unobtainable, so we let them drift out of our minds. And most people never let those desires interfere with immediate gratification. In other words, "Sure I'd like to have a million dollars, but you don't expect me to give up sitting on the couch binge watching Netflix to get it, do you?" If immediate gratification is more important than what you think you desire, maybe you really don't have a burning desire after all. Maybe it's just a "wouldn't it be nice if."

So, what's the difference between a "wouldn't it be nice if" and a Burning Desire? If it's just a "wouldn't it be nice if," you'd be content to lay on the couch and daydream about it...whereas a burning desire is something you'll jump up off the couch and give up binge watching Netflix for to go get it! Make sense?

## The Gnaw Factor

A true burning desire comes from deep inside yourself and when you think about it, it gets you excited and motivated. It has what I call the Gnaw Factor. I call it the Gnaw Factor because it gnaws at your inner self, trying to get out. It's something you've probably always known was there because you could feel it, but you've been afraid to let it out because it didn't fit your current life or with other people's plans for you.

For example; say you've always had a burning desire to be a musician, but your parents paid for law school because they wanted you to be a lawyer, so now you're a lawyer who never has time to even think about music. They got what they wanted but did you? Let me remind you, this is *your* life, not their's.

You only have one life to live. Now is the time to stop ignoring your burning desires that have been gnawing at you. Stop hiding them because you're not sure you can ever have them, or because you feel you don't deserve them, or that "they" (whoever they are) won't approve. You *can* have them, you *do* deserve them and attainment of your burning desire has nothing to do with what "*they*" want. The only thing that matters is whether or not it's something **you** want…something that gives you the Gnaw Factor.

Acknowledging a true burning desire is what gives you the confidence and power to not only take action but to act decisively and overcome anything that stands in your way of getting it. Rapper "Chika" acted on this much earlier than many adults. In an *InStyle* magazine article, she told a story about when she decided to drop out of school. She "came home one day and talked to my mom about wanting to be a musician and how it was a fire that was burning inside of me." She also took that time to "come out" to her mom. She acknowledged her burning desire which gave her the confidence to act decisively and tell her truth. She is so far ahead of the game by understanding at such a young age what it is to unapologetically "do her." One life to live…I'm just saying. And I see it all the time on shows like "America's Got Talent" where someone has been singing at home alone, isolated on some far off island for decades with mostly goats to talk to, and all of a sudden is standing on stage in another country being judged by Simon Cowell and over 3000 people. That takes a burning desire (and cojones). Acknowledging it is one of the keys to transforming your life from *just living*, to living your best life.

So, here's the big question for you.

## What are your Burning Desires?

## What has the Gnaw Factor for you?

Don't think you have any burning desires? I'll bet you do. The problem is that sometimes your burning desires have been hidden deep down for so long that even you have forgotten about them. Yes…that can happen.

It's ok. It may take a minute to be able to find *you* again. I'm asking the questions to help you find yourself and the hidden truths you may have felt you needed to bury inside for whatever the reason.

Let yourself think back in time if needed. In the next chapter you'll read about my story of thinking back in time. I had a twofer… rediscovering my hidden burning desire and finding my purpose in the process.

Meaning, think about what you were excited about being or doing before marriage and/or children, or your career put you and your desires on hold. There's nothing wrong with that of course, but we're circling back around to you now. This is your time, so let those desires that live deep within you…come back up to the surface. You're worth it. 100%.

> WE ALWAYS BELIEVE WHAT
> WE TELL OURSELVES.

##  Belief

You'll read more about the significance of burning desires throughout the book, but now let's discuss the second vital asset…Belief.

Beliefs are extremely powerful because we take actions on our beliefs both good and bad, and those actions can make or break your quality of life. Think about this…we may not always believe what others in our lives tell us, but somehow, **we always believe whatever we tell ourselves**. Sometimes that works for us and sometimes not so much. If you constantly emphasize a limiting belief, you start to believe it.

The beliefs we have about ourselves and our world come from everywhere; our parents growing up, people in our neighborhood, a church leader, or a schoolteacher.

Michelle Obama was told by a teacher to "lower her sights" implying she didn't have what it took to be successful. She said the teacher was planting a suggestion of failure before she even tried to succeed. I bet she wasn't the only kid her teacher told that to. Imagine how many kids were set up with limiting beliefs for life by that one person.

Michelle could've clung to that comment and made it a belief that kept her world small. But clearly, she was smart enough to ignore that voice of *un*-reason, and because of it…her world as we all know, definitely did *not* stay small. I wonder what kind of life that teacher has had. Hmmmmm.

Singer Cyndi Lauper had the exact opposite experience. She took her fourth-grade teacher's words of wisdom to heart and it's now her life motto; "Go forth and kick ass."

Words are powerful for better or worse.

Maybe your beliefs came from stories you heard when you were ear hustling adult conversations as a kid. Or maybe they came from family history trauma that you subconsciously held on to. That's the case with CNN reporter Anderson Cooper. He never expected to live past 50 so he didn't make plans for his life past that age. That belief came from his father dying at 50 so he believed he would too. On his 51$^{st}$ birthday he realized he had to figure out what to do with the rest of his life, since he actually still had one.

My late husband Richard…same thing. He was told no male in his family lived past 40, so he grew up expecting to die by 40. When he miraculously turned 40, he retired, bought a boat and sailed around the world for two years to celebrate. BTW, he lived until the age of 65 when he passed away from a motorcycle accident after saving a boy's life. He was living large those "extra" 25 years he grew up believing he wouldn't have.

Wherever they came from, beliefs are a powerful force of nature. **They're stubbornly etched in our brains until we decide to acknowledge them and get the *Etch a Sketch* out to erase them.** Now is the time for that *Etch A Sketch*.

## They Go Together

If you have a burning desire for something and you're not making progress toward it, chances are about 100% that you're missing the second asset… belief. You don't believe you can have it.

Here's a simple test to see if you believe or not. Let's say you have a burning desire to have all your debts paid and $50,000 in the bank. Say this aloud and firmly to yourself, "Within the very near future I have paid all my debts and have $50,000 in the bank." Now quickly, focus on the immediate thought that floods your mind. Did it make you feel good, like you can't even wait for it to happen or did you question it? Feel doubt? Laugh?

Say it again and this time really pay attention to your feelings. Are you still filled with a feeling of confidence that you're actually going to succeed, or are you still thinking more along the lines of "Yeah, so that's never going to happen"?

My hope is you felt excited and can't wait to make it happen, but don't worry if you were in the questioning and doubt group. That's more the norm, which is why this book exists. We'll take those limiting beliefs that are causing the doubt head on, one at a time to help you identify the source and give you the tools to *Etch A Sketch* them from your life.

# CHAPTER 5

# THE SWEET SPOT

*"My mother said to me, 'If you become a soldier, you'll be a general.
If you become a monk, you'll end up as the Pope.'
Instead, I became a painter and wound up as Picasso."*

Pablo Picasso

This is a big one. It's a bigger chapter because it's about Purpose which is a big subject.

## So, what is purpose, really?

Purpose is the answer to the 3 big questions in life.

Why am I here?
What does my life stand for?
What gives my life meaning?

No pressure there, right?

In my many years of mentoring people in coaching and seminars, the question of purpose is by far the biggest question I hear. So, if that's the case with you, just know that you're absolutely not alone.

If purpose is so important, why is it so hard to find? We briefly tap into it when we're young and asked, "What do you want to be when you grow up?" but then the treadmill of school and adulting happens. It's not talked about in school. There are no classes in vision or creating a purpose. Then we move on to a career, and for some, marriage and kids… and before you know it, you're reaching retirement and have never even thought of your purpose. If you did, you put it on the back burner because who has time for that in real life with real bills. You do what you need to get by. That's what Adulting is, right?

This chapter is to give you the mini class on purpose that you never got and that I wish I had earlier in life. If you *had* a purpose, I want to bring it back to the front burner. If you've *never* had one, I'm going to break this mystery down to see if you can finally get clear on finding yours. Either way, whatever your age, knowing your purpose will start you on a path to a more meaningful life.

> **I'M GOING TO BREAK THE MYSTERY DOWN.**

# The Sweet Spot

Burning desires usually coincide with purpose. The sweet spot is when your purpose and burning desire…and in some cases, destiny… align.

I say destiny because I feel some people are destined to do what they do. Like my dad. My father was a magnificent example of destiny, desire and purpose aligning. He knew in his pre-teens that he wanted to be a preacher, and a preacher he became. He was in ministry his whole life. Even after he retired, he went back to it because he missed it. My dad literally died sitting at his desk writing his sermon for the upcoming Sunday. He was living his purpose to the last second of his life.

Or think of Oprah Winfrey. Early in her career, Oprah was a news reporter/anchorwoman. She said she never felt comfortable in that role, and that she was always anxious, if you can imagine that. Then came the day when she co-hosted her first show in Baltimore, "People are Talking." That's when, in her words, it instantly felt like "I'd come home to myself. Not because the conversation was enlightening, but because of the feeling that at last I was where I was meant to be."

After 25 years, on the final episode of her mega success show, "Oprah," she told the audience she always "knew where I was meant to be when I was standing on that stage talking to viewers around the world. That was truly my **sweet spot**."

## What makes you feel that you are where you're meant to be? What is your "Sweet Spot?"

Don't know yet? It's OK. You'll get there.

If you do know, write it down to be a constant reminder to guide you as you make the intentional shift to get there.

## The Power Of 2nd Grade

I was always envious of my dad knowing at such a young age what he was meant to do. I questioned my purpose for decades and it bothered me to my core. "What's wrong with me? Why don't I know what my purpose is when some people know at like age 2, what their's is?"

I finally read something later in life that struck a chord and cleared it up for me. It was an article written about "purpose" by a career coach named Maureen Taylor. This piece gave me the "Aha" moment I needed.

Remember in the last chapter I spoke about thinking back in time? This is it.

She suggested you **think back to who you were in second grade because some psychologists believe it's around that age when we become our own individuals and tend to gravitate toward what makes us happy.**

That question prompted a flashback to me spending days in my room or up in my treehouse writing stories for hours and hours. I planned on being a writer because that's what I loved. No question. And at about the age of second grade, my wonderful encouraging mother who thought everything I wrote was brilliant, as mothers do, submitted my writings to *Readers Digest*, a popular magazine when I was growing up. That belief in me and my ability encouraged me even more and I continued to create with my words because it made me happy and more importantly to me as a child, it made her happy.

As I grew up and life happened, I got further and further away from writing. Then when Richard and I got together, I put *my* writing aside all together and became his editor and ghost writer… losing my writing voice to his.

After he passed away, I started writing again but I wasn't happy with anything I wrote. It just didn't feel right. In discussing it with my life coach, she helped me realize I was still writing in his voice. With that revelation, I became more aware and kept writing and rewriting until

I found my voice again. Now that I've found it, I haven't been able to stop writing.

This is my passion. I'm more driven now than I've ever been. This is the thing I will give up binge watching Netflix for, this is the thing I stay up until three in the morning without realizing it for. This is my sweet spot. And Boom, like that I'm living my purpose.

## The Big 3 Roadblocks

Now that I've told you about my journey to finding my purpose, I hope to help you find yours. Let's start with what's getting in the way. There are three main roadblocks to people finding their purpose.

1. Feeling it's too late in life for your purpose.

2. Feeling it has to be extraordinary.

3. Feeling you're supposed to have only one purpose in your whole life and it comes with divine intervention.

> THINK BACK TO WHO YOU WERE IN SECOND GRADE.

Any of those sound familiar?

Let me break down the myth of the big three for you.

 ## It's Never Too Late

It's been said that when what we're meant to do comes together in harmony with who we are, we become our truest, authentic self. You feel a shift.

My shift came from that suggestion to go back to my 2nd grade self to remember what I was passionate about back then. In doing so I unburied the truth I'd been hiding from myself for years, that writing is still my burning desire. It's so liberating to have finally re-discovered my passion and find my purpose *five decades* after elementary school!

I was the frickin' poster child for not knowing what my purpose was. I never thought I'd find it! So, if you don't know either, don't stress. I tell you my story to show you there's hope for you finding it. Don't feel intimidated by it or let it stop you from moving forward with your goals. I'll ask some prodding questions to help trigger it, and it'll eventually come to you. It's never too late.

On the TV show, "America's Got Talent," a former host of several entertainment TV shows auditioned. He had what many would say is a dream job interviewing celebrities, being on TV and making good money doing it, but he wasn't happy. He felt unfulfilled because he wasn't living his purpose.

His burning desire, his purpose, his sweet spot is to be a stand-up comic. He needed to leave his well-paying job for what he knew deep down inside he needed to feel complete. His wife supported him and a year later there he was on the other side of the camera auditioning in front of 4 celebrity judges that he had actually interviewed during his television career. He killed it. They loved it. He broke down and did the ugly cry because he had denied himself living his purpose for so long. It overwhelmed him to finally be living it. It was such a powerful moment that I was doing the ugly cry just watching it.

When my husband Richard was retired and on his boat in Rio, just drifting through life, literally…he had no purpose, no drive until he had the idea to revise *The Lazy Man's Way to Riches*. Then he suddenly had enough drive for three people. He was on fire. A fire inside of him that never burned out. Though he had made a lot of money in the past, he never felt like this. There was no ugly cry that I know of, just boundless energy and joy. This was his true purpose.

Point is…don't let where you are in the time of your life be a roadblock. Just pick it up and move it out of the way. You have things to do. It's never too late!

## 2  It Doesn't Have To Be An Extra-Ordinary Purpose

Another roadblock people put up is the feeling that purpose has to be some grand extraordinary thing that changes the world. It's true that for some, their purpose does mean achieving extraordinary things, like Martin Luther King who dreamed a dream and did what he could to make it happen. Or Representative John Lewis who continued fighting for that dream with passion and "good trouble" until his very last days.

But do all of us have to achieve these kinds of historical moments finding and fulfilling our purpose? Absolutely not. The meaning of the word *extra*ordinary means just that; very unusual or remarkable…*not* the ordinary. As Robert Kennedy pointed out: "Few will have the greatness to bend history itself, but each of us can work to change a small portion of events. It is from numberless acts of courage and belief that human history is shaped."

For some, your purpose can be the act of courage and belief of being the best supportive mother for your children to get them through life safely and as decent humans. If that's your purpose, please don't deny it because we need more descent humans in our world. Uh… I'm kind of messing up my own point because mothers are definitely extraordinary, but you get what I'm saying, right?

For some it could mean recognizing and working with the special and possibly extraordinary gifts that set you apart from others. Like Maya Angelou, who said of her purpose; "My mission in life is not merely to survive, but to thrive; and to do so with some passion, some compassion, some humor, and some style." Her purpose wasn't necessarily extraordinary but she and her gifts most definitely were.

Regardless of the scope of our purpose, finding out what our purpose is and pursuing it is what's really important to making our lives more meaningful.

 It Can Be More Than One And Doesn't Need Divine Intervention

I feel the biggest roadblock to discovering your purpose is looking for that ONE thing you think you're *supposed* to be and do. Like a word from your God himself saying this is your sole purpose for being alive. Damn, that's a lot of pressure to put on your God *and* yourself.

But that's probably the most common myth, and that limiting belief has caused emotional trauma for too many people for way too long. While it's true there are some people, as I mentioned earlier, that were just destined to do what they do, it's more the exception than the norm. The truth is you *can* have more than one purpose in your life. There isn't a period on your purpose. You can serve different purposes at different ages through different talents, so just *"Etch a Sketch"* that limiting belief away. Does that free you up at all?

## How Do You Discover It?
Now that we've discussed some of the more common things blocking you from finding your purpose, lets discuss

 the million-dollar question...
**How do I find my purpose?**

> **DON'T LET WHERE YOU ARE IN THE TIME OF YOUR LIFE BE A ROADBLOCK. JUST PICK IT UP AND MOVE IT OUT OF THE WAY. IT'S NEVER TOO LATE.**

First of all, I hate to break it to you, but you've probably had the answer inside of you all along. I did, but for many reasons, aka excuses, I had buried it for decades. I know I'm not the only one. I've had this discussion with many others who either personally denied their purpose or let someone in their life deny it for them, like a parent or a teacher. Did that happen with you?

Think back to when you were in school. A lot of people know early in their lives what they're meant to do. It shows itself early…like in second grade. There are times when it's more obvious for some, say the class clown that ends up becoming a comedian, like Jim Carrey.

I'm sure it's hard to believe but comedian and actor Jim Carrey was the class clown. To keep him from being a constant distraction, one of his teachers made a deal with him. If he behaved himself during the class, she would let him perform for the students at the end of every class. Everybody won. The teacher could teach and it gave him a place for his first stand up comedic performances.

Those moments when we're kids discovering our passions, are often stifled by a teacher or parent who thinks we're just going through a phase, or is doing it for you because they "want what's best for you." Problem is, it doesn't go away…it just gets buried deep down inside. And then there are those few, rare teachers like Jim was lucky enough to have, who recognize it and nurture it. Bless their hearts.

## Just "Listen" To Yourself...Not Others

That's why the question about second grade resonated with me so much. At that age we're filled with enthusiasm and energy for life and finding our passions. If any of that was stifled for you, the good news is you're grown now. You get to free yourself of *their* limitations, and decide what's best for you.

Sometimes you know deep down inside but ignore it and don't share it with anyone because when you do, you know you'll get everyone's opinion of why it's something you *can't* do… "You can't make enough money doing that. Go get a real job."

You need to stop listening to others and start listening to yourself.

What you want is deep within you! Start paying attention. It's been inside of you all the time and your conscious mind needs to finally hear it. Where does it come from? It comes from your inner soul, your subconscious. You'll learn more about your subconscious in a few chapters, but you know about "hunches." Hunches are creative thought from our subconscious that have weeded out the doubt we put in our conscious mind. Pay attention to your "hunches." What's important is to get in touch with your subconscious so you can hear it and then act on it.

The guy on "America's Got Talent" knew for years that this was his purpose. He denied it for a long time because he was making bank and wasn't ready to "go all in," but the Gnaw Factor got to him. It kept gnawing at his inner self until he did something about it.

When I paid attention, I realized my purpose… to write and bring awareness to others who may be struggling with something I've struggled with too, everything fell into place for that to happen.

> YOU'VE PROBABLY HAD THE ANSWER INSIDE OF YOU ALL ALONG.

## Trauma Or Experience

**Sometimes we don't find it…it finds us**, growing out of suffering, either our own or others. We just have to pay attention.

Saying that, I immediately think of the parents of the victims of #blacklivesmatter and #sayhername police killings. They and many supporters have a newly found purpose to make others aware of the egregious injustice of this violence and to try and initiate change through the Black Lives Matter and Say Her Name movements. Their purpose found them and they paid attention.

In the book *Second Acts*, Patricia Heaton tells the story of former Hollywood movie director Yudi Bennett who found her new purpose later in life. Her son was diagnosed with autism when he was 3. In middle school, her son was struggling until she discovered an afterschool animation program for kids with autism. A lightbulb went off for him in this program and he was a happier kid and better student because of it. Seeing this and having been a movie director, she developed a full time program to train young adults to be visual effects artists and animators culminating into a vocational school entitled *Exceptional Minds*. When the first class was ready to graduate, she decided to open her own production studio so her students could get work. Yudi took a traumatic life experience and made it into a purpose that changes lives and gives those young adults a chance for happiness. Her purpose found her and she paid attention.

And there's Generational Trauma. One of my best friends is a survivor of generational trauma and made a conscious decision to stop the pattern for her child. That's definitely a purpose that found her, but she took the controls. She became a therapist to help others navigate through it… and life.

Point is, Purpose builds upon your past experiences. Whoever you're meant to be evolves from where you've been and where you are now. It can be a buried burning desire like mine was, or it could be something that comes to you later in life through an experience.

The Japanese have the term IKIGAI, meaning… "A reason to live." Their theory is that your purpose…your reason for living, intersects between the four main areas of life;

## Passion: What you love

## Profession: What you're good at

## Mission: What the world needs

## Vocation: What you can be paid for

With that said, have you found your true calling? The reason you're alive? If so, you're one of the lucky ones. For those that are still looking, think about these four areas of life as you ask yourself the following questions.

① **What makes you want to leap out of bed each morning excited to get to it?**

② **What did you want to be in second grade?**

③ **What makes you feel that you're where you're meant to be?**

My hope is that this chapter and these questions provided triggers to help in answering this big as life question.

If you're still working through it, be patient. French Essayist Michel de Montaigne said, "The great and glorious masterpiece of man is to know how to live life on purpose."

Just remember, masterpieces take time.

# CHAPTER 6
# BURNING DESIRES INTO GOALS

*"Until you write down your dream, it is just a dream. Writing makes it a goal."*

John Goddard

*University of Illinois football coach Bob Zuppke was renowned for the fire and passion of his half-time pep talks. One afternoon, his team hit the locker room after the first half, well behind in both points and enthusiasm. Zuppke began talking to the team, and the more he talked the louder and more dramatic his voice became.*

*As he spoke, the momentum built in the players. Then coach pointed to the door at the far end of the locker room and said "Now go out there and win the game." Filled with emotion, the players got off the bench, ran towards the door and charged through it. But it was the wrong door, and one by one they fell into the school's swimming pool."*

Moral of the story, it's one thing to be all charged up…it's another to be headed in the right direction.

My father used that story in his sermon one day to the delight and roaring laughter of the congregation. It struck a chord with me because at that point in my life, I was filled with emotion, but going through a lot of wrong doors. I had no direction… no purpose.

Remember we talked about the two power principles; knowing what you want, and having a clearly defined plan written down to get it? This is where that gets defined, because **every day starts as a mistake if you don't know where you're going**. If you don't have a clear direction of where you want to go, you'll either stay stuck where you are, wander aimlessly or you'll go somewhere you didn't want to go, like falling into the proverbial swimming pool.

If setting goals is so critically important, why do so few people take the time to define their goals and map out where they want to go? I've discovered that the two most common reasons are due to confusion. First, confusion about how to properly set *clear* goals. Well, in these pages you'll learn how to clearly define your goals. Second, the confusion about the difference between Goals and Purpose. That's an easy one to clear up, right here and now.

> EVERY DAY STARTS AS A MISTAKE IF YOU DON'T KNOW WHERE YOU'RE GOING.

## Purpose Vs Goals

Simply put, "Purpose" is *where* to go, and "Goals" are *how* to get there.

Goals can be defined, reached and checked off a list, but they're just milestones along the way to your life's purpose. A purpose is *not* a goal. Your purpose can't be checked off a list like a goal. It's fulfilled continuously. Does that make sense? Let me give you a real-life example of what I'm talking about.

## The Worlds Greatest Goal Achiever

A friend of Richard's and mine was a man many called the real-life Indiana Jones. He was a world-famous adventurer and motivational speaker who is remembered as the **world's greatest goal achiever** among just a few of his life's accomplishments too long to list here.

John Goddard was the subject of many newspaper and magazine articles, as well as several TV shows, like "Dateline," which dedicated an episode to him and his accomplishments. This man was the real deal. If Instagram existed back then he would have millions of followers.

Here's where it all started. When he was fifteen, he overheard a friend of his parents bitching about the fact that "he wished he'd done more living when he was young because now he was too old." Limiting belief alert first of all because you're never too old, but the important part of this story is the fact that it made an immediate and lifelong impact on John. It inspired him to never have a life of regrets, so that same day he sat down and wrote three words at the top of a yellow legal pad… "My Life List." That list is now a world-famous list used in motivational books and speeches about goal setting all over the world and is considered to be the original "bucket list."

## The Original Bucket List

The list John wrote down that day at 15 years young was filled with 127 clearly defined, detailed goals of things he wanted to do in his life. And not just any goals. Some of the most unbelievable goals anyone could come up with, such as No. 91…watch a cremation ceremony in Bali. Who does that? Who even knows that's a thing at 15? A boy with a purpose, that's who.

John is the one who wrote and lived the quote at the start of this chapter; "Until you write down your dream, it is just a dream. Writing makes it a goal." Well, he certainly not only wrote down his goals, he spent his life going after each and every one of them with gusto. Each goal was meticulously checked off as he reached it and then he would move on to another one. When he passed away from cancer at 88 years old, he had lived one of the most incredible lives of anyone I've ever heard of, and had accomplished all but a couple of his original 127, as well as some he added to the list along the way. The few he didn't get to cross off his list weren't due to his limitations, but the world's, like landing on the moon. Whatever the final number of goals achieved was, it was about 125 more than most people will ever try in a lifetime.

John's purpose in life was "To Be, To Do, To See." **He checked off over 125 goals** *along the way* **to his purpose.**

## Direction vs. Defined Goals

Whatever your goals are, you're ahead of most people already because you've started the self-evaluation process of deciding where you want to go and identifying your burning desires. But most people stop here if they even make it this far. They think because they've made their lists, they're good to go. But what they have is a direction…not a goal.

Let me explain the difference. An example between a direction and a defined goal is the difference between say, the simple compass *direction* of "west" …and the detailed *explanation* of, "the entrance to the west rim of the Grand Canyon." One is merely a direction; the other is a definite location. Make sense?

If you don't have focus and direction, it becomes all too easy to remain in analysis paralysis in your mind without any real effort to make it happen.

Imagine the completely different life John would've had if he just made the list, then hung it up on his mirror because he wanted to decide what to do first and then put the new list in order, then alphabetize it…whatever procrastination tactic, instead of taking immediate action and going after each one and living a life that few can even imagine.

So, having said that, direction for the goal *is* important. If you don't have direction you can get lost getting to the west rim of the Grand Canyon.

But it's the detail of how the goal is worded that's the most critical aspect. **A goal correctly stated is specific, clearly defined, measurable and in absolute terms.** Meaning, at any point, if you are asked if you have achieved your goal, you need to be able to give a definitive "yes" or "no" answer. For example, you can give a definitive answer to whether or not you're currently standing at the entrance to the west rim of the Grand Canyon. Get it? That's the level of clarity you need in order to form a goal that your mind can lock onto and move towards.

#1 on Johns list was to explore the Nile. He could definitively say he did that. He actually kayaked down the Nile. Yes, the complete 4132 miles of the Nile with all the wild animals like Hippos and Crocodiles that were alongside of him trying to kill him as he did it. Goal checked off, while living his purpose… To Be, To Do, To See.

And finally, **define your goal as if it already happened.** It's been said that the best way to predict the future, is to create it. So, create an amazing future like he did by writing it down.

You'll see a significant difference once you've established clear, committed, measurable goals. In 1954, Yale University did a study that found that only 3% of the graduating seniors had clear written goals. Twenty years later, in 1973, the surviving members of that class were interviewed, and it was found that the 3% with clear written goals was worth more in financial terms than the other 97% combined. Cha-Ching$. Though the study was a long time ago, the concept is just as valid today. Goal setting worth it? 100%!

## Your Goals

So, you may not be ready to write a Life List like John's, but you can create your own list. And if John's story *did* inspire you to write a more adventurous life list, go for it! Now's the time! Go Be, Go Do, Go See!

You learned that it's the detail of how the goal is worded that is what really makes the difference, right? So, as you're creating yours, think about the things on your wants, needs and personality qualities lists we talked about in chapter three and use the following 7 question checklist to make sure they're worded properly and are consistent with you, your purpose and your life.

( 1 ) **Do you really want this?** Or is it something someone else wants you to achieve?

( 2 ) **Does this goal contradict any other goal you're setting?** Is your burning desire to be a pre-school teacher but you've listed a goal of a million-dollar house with a Rolls Royce in the garage? They may be contradicting each other. Know what I'm saying?

( 3 ) **Is your goal stated as a positive rather than a negative?** Is it what you want, as opposed to what you want to get rid of? "I am 50 pounds lighter and feel healthy" vs. "I need to lose 50 pounds." Make sense?

**(4) Is your goal in graphic detail?** Dollar amounts, colors, etc.

**(5) Is the goal high enough?** Be sure those limiting beliefs don't creep in and limit your goal setting.

**(6) Are you including the personality qualities needed for goal achievement?** Such as Self-Confidence and a Do it Now attitude.

**(7) Is each goal stated as though already accomplished?** I have... I own... I am...!

## It Ok To Make Adjustments

BTW...it's ok if your goals change throughout this process. That's normal. This is all about you, and your vision will get clearer and sharper as you go through this process.

Think about this...when a commercial airliner flies from one city to another, it's off course over 90% of the time. It just keeps measuring it's

## DEFINE YOUR GOAL AS IF IT'S ALREADY HAPPENED.

progress and adjusting it's heading over and over again to stay on the right path to the destination. Goal setting works the same way. It allows you to see clearly what you need to do every day in order to keep yourself moving in that direction. The most important thing here is you're taking action to move forward, and course correct as you do it.

**CHAPTER 7**

# TOP 10 LIST TO TURN YOUR GOALS INTO REALITY

*"A goal is created three times; First as a mental picture...
second when written down for clarity and dimension...
and third when you take action towards its achievement."*

Gary Ryan Blair

When asked during an interview how he managed to reach the top as a professional bodybuilder, become a famous movie star, and former Governor of California, Arnold Schwarzenegger replied with a single word, "Drive!"

People like Arnold with an intense burning desire to achieve their goals are referred to as "driven." Is this a special quality only for a privileged few? Absolutely not. Any one of us can become "driven" if our goal is a true burning desire and not just a "wouldn't it be nice if."

So how do you nurture and achieve those goals? You make changes to your current attitude and environment in ways that'll set you up for success. With that in mind, I'm going to give you 10 steps towards achieving any goals you set for yourself…but first I'll go over the three ways to NOT realize your goals, to clear those roadblocks from the start.

## How *Not* To Realize Your Goals

These are the 3 most common ways people set themselves up for failure.

 AIM AT NOTHING!

The problem here is when you aim at nothing, you'll hit it every time and you end up with nothing. This is those that *talk about it* but never get off the couch to *be about it*. All you'll get from this approach is a big couch potato ass and possibly a beer belly.

 AIM AT EVERYTHING!

This method is for those who just go for anything hoping something sticks. Yeah…no. That doesn't work and yet is a strangely popular one.

 AIM AT THINGS!

"Things" are good, so setting goals to get "things" you want is not a bad thing. But if that's the *only* kind of goals you're setting, then you my friend are shallow, and we need to work on your character development. Oh wait…we are.

You may see your past behavior in one of these three, but remember, you're learning to be un-common, so you won't be doing these anymore. I'm just listing them as a reminder of what *not* to do. Now on to the positive action. Ten steps you can take to achieve any goals you set for yourself.

# Top Ten Steps To Realize Your Goals

 KNOW WHAT YOU WANT

The good news is you've already aced this one! If you are reading intentionally, you've already gone through the hard work of identifying what it is you want, need and have a burning desire for.

 WRITE YOUR GOALS DOWN IN DETAIL

Nice. You've aced this one too. You've already learned this and have written out clear detailed goals stated in a positive, already achieved format. Boom! Next.

 TAKE IMMEDIATE ACTION...

Writing down your goals is the first step to making it a reality, but just seeing it on paper isn't going to get you there. Once you set a goal, immediately do something towards getting it.

Don't worry so much about making the *long-term* detailed plans to get there because that can hold you back. It's true that the *goal itself* needs to be written in detailed form, but the detailed *plan* to get the goal achieved can be hashed out a little later. Why?

Because too often people get stuck in the state of analysis paralysis and never reach the action stage because they're going for the big red-carpet production the first time out. You can be all charged up and raring to go like the football team you read about in Chapter Six, but if you sit there in the locker room going over and over the plays waiting for the Superbowl, but never open the door to go out on the field to play the season games, you're not going to win anything. The goal to be achieved keeps getting delayed due to the *planning* for the goal which never gets completed. Make sense?

Action is the most important part of the plan so, remember, start where you are, with what you have and build from there. Don't wait for anyone… just do it yourself! Take baby steps to get to the bigger steps. Identify the very first physical action you need to take, and then do it! It will help build confidence and momentum for the next step. Whatever the situation, don't just talk about it…*Be* about it. Because if you don't make a conscious effort to work on your goals, you'll end up back working on other people's goals.

## …THE RIGHT ACTION

Just as important as taking action is…taking the *right* action. Get up to dominate the day! Start your day with a morning routine to set yourself up for success. At the start of the day think…What is the result producing activity towards my goal that *only I* can do?

If it's a personal goal of say, losing weight, start your day off with a morning walk before anything else so you know you've accomplished something first thing towards your goal. It sets you up for success the rest of the day.

If it's a business goal, don't "major in the minors." Meaning don't get caught up straightening the office supply cabinet when your office manager can be doing that. Spend your time doing what only you can do to take a step closer to your goal. If you are your own office manager and have to do that task, do it after hours, after you've been productive doing the more important business.

If you're an entrepreneur, do what activity you can that will lead you to making more money for your business.

If you're not working right now as many people aren't, your immediate action needs to be finding a way to work in this new normal we find ourselves in, or rediscovering your passion so you can make a decision on what direction you want to go next.

Whatever your situation, think of this sobering question to keep you on point… Steve Jobs, founder of Apple used to look in his mirror every morning and ask himself this question; **"If today were the last day of my life, would I want to do what I'm about to do today?**

 ## BURN YOUR SHIPS

Here's action for you…Have you ever heard the expression, "He *burned that ship* a long time ago?"

In 334 BC, Alexander the Great led a fleet of Greek and Macedonian ships across the Dardanelles Straits into Asia Minor. When he reached the shore, he ordered his men to burn the ships. By burning the ships, Alexander hoped to motivate his troops to fight to survive. He told his men, "We will either return home in Persian ships or we will die here." Now that's action and commitment supersized.

If your goals are important enough to you, then you can start by burning the proverbial ships, so you have no choice but to go for it. In other words, let go of your safety net. For example, if your dream is to quit work and launch your own business, you can begin by making the commitment to quit your j-o-b. Write a letter of resignation, and put it in an envelope with a date on it for when you commit to yourself to handing it in. I'd make the date short term to motivate yourself and set a reminder in your calendar.

If you don't burn those ships, you've just sent another message to your subconscious mind that it's OK to quit your goal. And when the going gets tough, as it inevitably does for any worthwhile goal, you'll quit once again. If you really want to achieve your goals, then you've got to burn those ships to the ground. If you're thinking that sounds extreme, that the average person won't do this, you're right…but that's why *they're* stuck in an average life.

 ## VISUALIZE IT

When asked how he accounted for his amazing inventive genius, Thomas Edison replied, "It's because I never think in words, I think in pictures." This is one of those not so secret power plays that successful people do. Motivational speaker, author and Law of Attraction teacher Bob Proctor said, "If you see it in your mind, you're going to hold it" because our minds think in images, like Edison realized.

Have you taken the time to "see" what it's going to look like when your goal is accomplished?

The actor and comedian Jim Carrey visualized it and did affirmations, which we'll talk about in several chapters. He would visualize the things he wanted as being his, including acting jobs. He visualized having directors interested in him and people he respected saying they liked his work.

But the best part of this story is he did what I've been preaching… he wrote it down. He wrote himself a check for $10 million for acting services rendered and gave himself three years to "cash" it. He dated it Thanksgiving 1995 and put it in his wallet where it stayed and kept deteriorating. Then just before Thanksgiving 1995, he found out that he was going to make $10 million on the movie "Dumb and Dumber." True story. Not so dumb Jim Carrey. Perfect example of visualizing your goal.

Visualize your goal already obtained like Jim did. Visualize yourself living it; taste it, feel it, smell it, see it, cash the check. As an example; if tangible like a goal of a new car…go car shopping for the dream car you want to buy. Sit in it. Smell the leather and new car smell. Visualize the Vanity License plate you'll have. Take a picture of yourself sitting in it to keep on your desk for visual motivation.

I'm sure you've heard the term "Fake it until you make it." That's what you're doing. Imagine yourself as **you're going to be** when that goal is achieved and keep that picture in your mind.

> What are you envisioning for yourself right now? Write it down.

 # CHANGE YOUR HABITS

I have a chapter devoted to it later, but to state the obvious, you need to make changes to things you're currently doing, to see the changes you want.

You know as well as I do that hanging on to one or more of your bad habits gets in the way of reaching your goals. Say you have a goal of losing 15 pounds but stop at Mickey D's for a Quarter Pounder with cheese, fries and a coke every night on the way home from work. Bad habits getting in the way much? You're setting yourself up for failure, and you know it, which adds to your frustration and low self-esteem causing an endless cycle.

So why don't we change? Because those habits are comfortable, even if they make your life *un*-comfortable. Most people are more afraid of change, even good change, than being uncomfortable. Sounds a bit crazy when you read it though, right? Make the change. **Take your control back** to reach the goals you've set for yourself. You can do it. Baby steps.

 # STOP SELF-BULLYING

This is one of the worst habits people get into and one of the universal roadblocks to achieving goals. You can do all the steps I've mentioned, but if you constantly tell yourself that you're not worthy, either consciously or subconsciously, it's going to stop you in your tracks from getting everything you want. We'll talk about this more in Chapter Sixteen but just remember this… **we always believe what we tell ourselves.**

You are the creator of your thoughts and the one responsible for holding on to your beliefs, so you're the one with the power to, at any moment, change your thoughts, beliefs and self-talk to life enhancing rather than self-limiting.

## Quit the self-verbal abuse...the self-bullying. Believe you're worthy. You are.

### 8) REMOVE THE TOXIC PEOPLE

Just as you can choose to stop being toxic to yourself, you also have the right to remove the toxic people in your life. You know... those people that should come with a warning label! The ones that tell you there's no way you can ever achieve that goal and seem to go out of their way to make sure you don't.

It's been said that you can see your future just by looking at the six people you spend the most time with. Made you immediately start thinking of who you hang around with, right? Good. Really think about it. Write their names down. If you don't like what you see, cross them off the list and let those people go. There's no honor in remaining loyal to people who expect and even want you to fail.

Toxic people are my pet peeve. I discuss them throughout the program and Chapter Eighteen is devoted to saying "Bye Felicia!" You need to remove the toxic and negative people from your life, or you're wasting your time here. They will always try to hold you back and make you feel small. They need to go. Say "Bye Felicia" and move on. Period. Control, Alt, Delete!

### 9) BUILD YOURSELF A NEW SUPPORT SYSTEM

As you get rid of the toxic people in your life, replace them with people who are going to be a positive, supportive influence. Build a support system that will help you move in the right direction you've chosen. Find a friend who "gets" you, will support you in a positive way and will tell you about yourself if you start backtracking.

Comedian and Actress Kym Whitley calls her tribe "The Opinion" because they all have their own opinion about what she should or shouldn't be doing. But that's what she wanted. She has them to keep her accountable and on the right track, and whether they agree with her or not, they always support her. That's the kind of support I'm talking about. Your "ride or die" tribe.

If there's no one in your life that can support you, or no one who understands where you want your goal to take you, talk to a professional counselor, life coach, teacher or pastor.

One of the best ways to have support is in a community of people on the same path to their best life. There are plenty of support groups and networking groups out there, including our own private online community @nopermissionsociety. More information on that at the end of the book.

Find a mentor. Play with better players in whatever your interest or goal is in. Learn from those playing the game at the highest level possible. Don't ask a broke friend how to get rich. Know what I'm saying?

# 10 ) CREATE A MORNING AND EVENING ROUTINE FOR SUCCESS

Finally, I suggested in #3 of this chapter that you get up to dominate the day and start your day with a positive action to set you up for success towards your goal. I also have a suggestion for the end of the day: take a few minutes to review your day. Did you do something towards achieving your goals…or get stuck helping others achieve theirs?

You'll notice after the first day how it sharpens your focus and makes you think about how you're spending your day. **When you end the day, if you feel that you lived it the same way you would if you had a chance to repeat it…**then you gain a sense of empowerment that helps you keep your focus for the next day, and the next, and the next.

## Next Level

The steps I mentioned above are what any ordinary person can do to achieve their goals. But I want you to be *extra*-ordinary. So, now I'm going to give you the secret that was the basis for Joe Karbo's success, for Richard's success, mine and many others around the world. You've earned it. You've worked hard to get here.

The next four chapters are what helped us all go next level. It's finally time to share this powerful Lifehack that has been used by geniuses for hundreds of years to get everything they wanted.

## Are you ready?

# IT'S THE LAW!

*"What you think, you become…
What you feel, you attract…
What you imagine, you create."*

Buddha

With the first seven chapters, we've been building your foundation…your "someplace." Now you get to learn the secret to Joe's original success. The thing that helped him and those that have followed, go from ordinary to *extra*-ordinary.

This is the lifehack that you'll use to get everything you've been putting down on those lists, whether mental or written down, and get to your "someplace."

The secret I'm talking about, the law Joe used to put all of his powerful principles of success into practice is something he called Dyna/Psyc.

## So, What Is This Law?

Do you remember the book and movie *The Secret* about the natural laws of science called the Law of Attraction? It became a big deal, as it should because the Law of Attraction works. It's still 100% relevant and continues trending on Netflix.

Joe Karbo wrote about The Law of Attraction long before *The Secret*, he just called it something different. Dyna/Psyc is the term he created when referring to the collection of natural laws that make up this success formula. But it's all the same principle: The Law of Attraction…like attracts like… that what you want, wants you.

I will show you how to use **the law of attraction to find the hidden untapped power within yourself to attract, or manifest what it is you want.**

Celebrity Steve Harvey sums it up even better; "Like attracts like. You are a magnet. Whatever you are, that's what you draw to you. If you're negative, you're going to attract negativity. If you're positive, you attract positivity. If you see it in your mind, you can hold it in your hand."

> LIKE ATTRACTS LIKE. YOU ARE A MAGNET. WHATEVER YOU ARE, THAT'S WHAT YOU DRAW TO YOU.

Your mind, the subconscious in particular, has tremendous power over you. Look at Buddha's quote at the beginning of this chapter. "What you think… you become. What you feel…you attract. What you imagine… you create." That is the Law of Attraction. It's about manifesting what you want, hence the lists!

## It Used To Be A Secret…Literally.

This universal law has been around since biblical days, but back in the 1950's, key executives of big, highly successful corporations began to be made aware of it. At that time it was called the Scientific Basis of Success, the study of natural laws applied to create success.

We've come a long way since then. Since those early days, research has continued and certain well-defined patterns of power that lead to success became obvious…and more well known.

Now, successful people from athletes to business people to celebrities have embraced these natural laws and learned to use them to their advantage. Besides Steve Harvey, actor and rapper Will Smith is among the many celebrities that feel the Law of Attraction is the key behind their success. And great athletes like Michael Jordan and Muhammad Ali learned to master the use of the laws and bring to reality what they first created in their own mind.

## You'll Learn To "Plug In"

Can you learn how to apply the Law of Attraction to your life? Absolutely! We're all born with the same potential to achieve success and *everything* we want in our lives. The power to make things happen has always been available. It's learning to plug in to the existing power, the natural sources from the Universe that makes the difference.

I use the analogy of plugging in, because the forces of the Law are like electricity. No one invented electricity; it existed in nature. But, until man learned how to make use of the already existing natural phenomenon, we had no electric lights to turn night into day.

Now anyone can perform that miracle with the flick of a switch because we know how to "plug in" to the electricity. Get it? You're going to learn to do the same thing with this already existing natural law.

In the last chapter we talked about affirmations and visualization. In the next few chapters, we'll discuss those and other techniques you'll be learning to use to put these powerful natural laws to work for you.

I know this is a lot of new concepts for you to process. Just believe the possibility that it might work for you. What do you have to lose? Author Bob Proctor says, "The Law of Attraction is always working whether you believe it or understand it or not." I was skeptical when I first learned of it myself, but Richard was living proof that using this practice worked. Everything he wanted, he got. Everything he *even thought* about wanting, he got, but that's part of the secret.

So seeing it worked for him, I started paying attention and researching it, and discovered the great geniuses of our time used this power as well. You'll read more about that in the next chapter, but point is it works and has since the beginning of time. I soon learned to use it for myself and my life has been better because of it. 100%. I ask for what I want and need, and it comes to me. I manifest it. It's honestly as simple as a mind shift and being open to the possibilities. And with it, the possibilities are endless.

**Remember I told you that you would need an open mind? Now is the time to try something new and believe.**

# THE ULTIMATE MINDHACK

*"More gold had been mined from the thoughts of men than has been taken from the earth."*

Napoleon Hill

*Burt Rutan shot out of bed one morning and sketched the plans to a re-entry technique that came to him while he was sleeping. The key innovation he had to sketch that morning was a tail that folds up when the ship reaches space. The re-entry plans were for his "SpaceShipOne", the first privately developed spacecraft. The hinged tail that came to him in a dream helped him win the $10 million Ansari X Prize for sending "SpaceShipOne" into suborbital flight twice in a two-week period.*

## What Is Your SubCom?

Your SubCom is the ultimate mindhack. What is it? Your subconscious computer. Let me explain.

Have you ever had something you were struggling with or were trying to decide and said, "Let me sleep on it?" That's using your subconscious computer. Burt Rutan "slept on it" and made history and bank!

Many dreams allow us to *see* things before they happen. The ancient Hebrews said that we partake in the wisdom and prescience of the Gods when we're asleep. You can use this power of subconscious intelligence no matter what your faith, or even if you don't have faith. It's not a religious thing…it's a science thing.

## Rewrite The Code And Be A Genius

You'll discover that the subconscious is a great source of wisdom by allowing access to deeper levels of self-awareness. In the classic book, *The Man Who Tapped the Secrets of the Universe,* the author tells us the words of the genius sculptor Walter Russell. He said, "I believe that mediocrity is self-inflicted, and that genius is self-bestowed. Every successful man I have ever known carries with him the key which unlocks that awareness and lets in the universal power that has made him into a master."

What is the key? **The master key is learning to create conscious access to your subconscious computer.**

I call it the ultimate mind hack. Sir John Hargrave said we can hack back into our minds and rewrite the code. Well, that's what we're doing by using the subconscious computer. You'll use your subconscious computer (SubCom) strategically, to rewrite your code and build a mindset that will help you level up for life. You're going to bestow genius upon yourself.

Many of the people we consider to be geniuses used this power. Albert Einstein used to spend time "daydreaming" which he said he used for problem solving.

> YOU GET TO CLAIM WHO YOU WANT TO BE.

Painter Salvador Dali used his subconscious computer creatively to come up with new ideas for his paintings. And Thomas Edison not only accessed his subconscious computer to work through problems, he taught his staff to do it too. Innumerable other inventors, scientists, writers, and composers have given evidence of their using the great subconscious computer that exists in all of us.

The brilliant inventor, futurist and engineer Nikola Tesla, who The Tesla Motor Company is named in tribute to, said his subconscious computer gave him the ideas for all his inventions. When an idea for an invention came to his mind, he would build it in his imagination…visualizing… knowing that his subconscious would reveal to his conscious mind all the parts needed to make it a reality. By doing that, he didn't have to go through numerous rebuilds because he had already "seen" it and worked out all the kinks in his subconscious. He said it worked every time. We'll never know for sure if his claim is true, but I know the power of the subconscious so I would say it didn't hurt him any.

## It's All Real

Besides geniuses, the science community has learned that your subconscious mind doesn't know the difference between imagination and reality. **It's *all* real to the subconscious mind.** It doesn't make a distinction between real and made up, or between destructive and constructive thoughts. Re-read that paragraph, it's a game changer.

**In reprogramming your subconscious, you get to claim who you *want* to be.** It's literally a mind shift. When you put your goal into your subconscious mind as though its already true, the subconscious gets it, after repetition the *conscious* mind gets it and presto whamo, your goal is achieved. Genius, right?

So now knowing that, let's talk about that master key…learning to create conscious access to it. You've actually been using it, you just didn't know it.

## Pay Attention To You

Think about this, have you ever noticed yourself pulling into a parking spot at work and don't even remember driving there? That was your subconscious computer working on auto pilot. You were so busy with your conscious thoughts that your subconscious computer kicked in to get you to work.

Or when a name was "on the tip of your tongue" but you couldn't think of it, haven't you told someone "I'm sure I'll think of it on the way home?" And then, just as you said you would, you remembered it later? That too was an example of the use of this power.

Now that you're aware of it…pay attention to *you*. Your subconscious computer will suggest moves, ideas, and strategies to you. Be responsive to your own ideas. Every time you had a "hunch" that solved a problem for you, you were using this power. We often discount our hunches, slips of the tongue, or the messages we get through dreams, but it can protect you if you listen to it. Sometimes, as in dreams, the subconscious mind is offering confirmation or validity to something going on in your current life that you may not even consciously be aware is a problem. Be alert and ready to receive.

## Danger Will Robinson
*( TV show "Lost in Space" reference)*

A recurring dream is important because it may warn you about something you might be dealing with. Your subconscious is saying stop, look and listen. Listen to your gut. I read about a woman who had a recurring dream for several nights in a row. In her dream she saw a high mountain impossible to climb, in-between her fiancé and herself. The mountain signified an unsurmountable obstacle, but she couldn't think of anything that was blocking their relationship. Her therapist suggested she talk to her fiancé to see if he was hiding anything from her.

He finally admitted he was gay and was only marrying her to keep his religious business customers from pulling their business which they would do if he were to "come out."

That's cold. He was willing to ruin both of their lives because he didn't have the uh…nerve to come out as gay. Thankfully she listened to her gut, her SubCom, and saved herself from a marriage that would've been unfulfilling for both of them and would've blocked her fiancé's authentic self. That's a very specific example but it makes the point doesn't it? Pay attention.

## Problem Solved

Like Burt, those people who, when faced with an important decision or a problem to be worked out, decide to "sleep on it" and awaken the next day with the answer, are unknowingly using their subconscious computer. I've used my SubCom for years. I awaken so many times with the answer to a problem or a new idea for a book, that I keep a small notepad on my nightstand so I can capture it before my conscious mind kicks in and I forget it.

Author John Steinbeck said "It's a common experience that a problem difficult at night, is resolved in the morning after a committee of sleep has worked on it." Here's how to make the committee of sleep work for you. There are three key words for putting your subconscious to work specifically on problems: **WRITE, TRY, ASK**

 WRITE

A lot of problems stay rattling around in your head like a cluster because they haven't been clearly defined, so using the same concept as writing down your goals, write down your *problem*. Start with the words, "Should I do this. . . ?" and write out the problem just as detailed as you did your goals.

 TRY

Sometimes just getting it out of your head and seeing it on paper gives you clarity. If not, try to answer it yourself. You've heard about writing the Pros' and Con's in certain situations? That's what you'll do here if it's a decision to be made. Two columns; in one column put all the reasons for taking the particular step. In the other, all the reasons against. If you still can't come up with the answer…

 ASK

Ask the Universe. Ask for what you want…in this case, your subconscious computer to solve it for you. I know it sounds a bit cray-cray but it's for real. Read on.

Here's an example of asking your SubCom to solve your problems for you, taken from Patricia Heaton's book *Your Second Act*. Former football player Ta'u Pupu'a was living his dream playing in the NFL for the Cleveland Browns when a 370-pound teammate landed full force on his foot, crushing his arch. After taking a year to recover from that he was injured again. His football career was over. He asked the Universe… "What am I supposed to do?" An answer came back to him to "move to New York, go sing." I'm sorry…What?

Well, he listened to his SubCom and did just that. He started with what he had…a suitcase and a $100 bill from his grandmother, and built from that. He used the lessons he learned in his football career to study the successful people doing what he wanted to do. He got a job at the restaurant across the street from the Met Opera house and Julliard school of music and would ask questions to all the performers who dined there.

Eventually he landed a small non-paying role with a small opera company. One night, he waited an hour to meet a Soprano who is Polynesian like himself, and she ended up helping him get an audition for a Julliard scholarship.

Three years later, he made his professional debut with the San Francisco Opera and he's never looked back. His subconscious computer answered his question regarding his problem, and here's the important part…he paid attention and took action without questioning it. The law of attraction provided the rest...*and* he found his true purpose. That's how it works.

So, try it. Think of your subconscious as another person, or committee. Just say to that force that you want the answer to the problem and then let it go, because once you've asked the subconscious computer to solve it for you, your computer won't work on a problem while you're consciously working on it.

## How Will I Know Its Working?

This is hard to explain but...listen to your gut, you'll just know. You'll feel it. I'm sure you've experienced this at some point in your life. When you *just know* you've found the right house to buy, or you *just know* when you find the love of your life. *You'll just know...* like Burt did jumping out of bed to sketch his idea.

So, when you've asked your SubCom for help, be on the alert. Stay aware. The answers can come to you in the most unusual, random ways. Something may keep coming to your mind, in connection with the problem, but it won't be an *obvious* connection. For me it's music. I'll get a song in my mind that won't go away and eventually I realize it's relevant to a problem I've had. Weird but true; because music is how I pay attention.

## Subconscious Mind Hack # 1: The Grown-Up Time Out

Another essential part of using this powerful mind hack is to learn to relax and release stress. Your conscious mind holds on to memory, habits, self-image and all the limiting beliefs you tell yourself... all the negative things you may have been told growing up that you've held on to. When you're relaxed, you're more receptive and therefore able to release to your subconscious, and your mind is able to filter out all the crap you feed it.

So mindhack #1 is something called the "grown-up time out"! The grown-up time out is a time out for yourself, but unlike a child's time out used as punishment, this is a good thing. It's a brief restorative time when you can just stop thinking for 10-15 minutes and give your mind a refresh. It's a power nap without the nap part.

Oprah calls it her peaceful pause. She gives herself a time out at least once a day, and twice when she's on point. Twenty minutes in the morning and twenty minutes at night. She says that stillness is the space where all creative expression, peace, light, and love come to be. Yeah…that.

I can almost hear the panic. You're thinking… "Sure, Oprah is a billionaire, of course she has time, but I live in the real world and have absolutely no time for this." People from the beginning of time have complained about not having enough time, but especially in today's world where it seems every minute of the day is scheduled with something. And yet, you'll find people's heads buried in their phone or tablet for hours mindlessly looking at cat videos on social media or creating puppy faces in Snap Chat or obsessing over someone's Insta life. I've even seen babies staring at screens. It's become a massive time suck.

So, if you re-think it with those things in mind, I think you can find time for you. If you pay attention to where your time is spent, I think you'll be able to shave off 20 minutes here or there for your sanity and life refresh. I've heard from other readers that found time by shutting themselves in

> OPRAH CALLS IT HER PEACEFUL PAUSE.

the bathroom, or getting to work or the school carpool lane early to sit in the car for their grown-up time out. Actress Charlize Theron says her child calls her bath time, mommy's time out. That's an ideal place for a Grown-Up Time Out. Calgon take me away! (old commercial reference for those of you that don't know.)

## Learn To Be Silent

Wherever you find those minutes, I realize trying to be silent, even for brief pockets of time is something you may need to learn. Try 10 minutes first. Not gonna lie, those 10 minutes might drag on a bit at first until you learn to find your quiet place.

Martha Beck, a writer and contributor to Oprah's magazine wrote about a study done on "free" time. In the study, researchers gave the subjects 15 minutes to either sit quietly or press a button that would give them an electric shock. There was no upside to pressing the button. The choice was 15 minutes of stillness or mild pain.

Now it seems obvious doesn't it, that any sane person would choose the 15 minutes of free time over being shocked? Yeah, no. Shockingly, (see what I did there), two thirds of the men and a quarter of the women, all of whom had previously said that they would pay money *not* to be shocked, chose self-torture over sitting with their thoughts. One person pressed the button 190 times! Really?

We're programmed to get up and do something 24/7, pre-pandemic anyway, but for your peace of mind, learn to be silent. No matter how uncomfortable you are at first, stay there for the full time. You'll learn to crave those silent treatments. Trust.

You get to be in control of where you journey to in your mind to find peace. So, in your mind, go to the place where you have perfect peace every time you think of it. It could be the mountains with a babbling brook, for me it's my happy place in Southern California that I go ocean kayaking.

It's amazing how quickly your body can respond to the time-out. Once you get used to being silent, you'll experience automatic relaxation and stress will vanish, allowing a pathway to open up your subconscious. You'll find increased enthusiasm, energy, and an overall increase in your sense of well-being. New and creative ideas will just seem to "come from nowhere." For real.

Another side benefit is that you'll now know how to make it available when you need it. I use it when I'm having writers block. I take time out to give my mind a rest from all the clutter in my head blocking my words getting on to paper, and after my Grown Up Time Out, the words come back to me every time.

So, here's how the Grown-Up Time Out works;

- **Make a conscious decision to take the uninterrupted time for you.** Put your phone on silent and set it upside down or in a pocket so the screen light doesn't distract you.

- **Sit down and simply close your eyes.** Relax, but don't go to sleep. Remember this is the power nap without the nap part. Just let go and take a peaceful pause.

- **Make this a part of your daily routine for Success.** Do it at least once a day. Twice is better. 20 minutes in the morning and 20 minutes in the evening. Put it in your schedule as an appointment if necessary. No one needs to know the appointment is with yourself.

In the next two chapters, you'll read about the other powerful mindhacks that you'll use the SubCom to complete. But as a final thought on this one, here's a fun and fitting retro movie reference.

In one of the Star Wars movies, Luke Skywalker needed to do something immediately that was seemingly impossible, that he wasn't trained for and didn't have the skills for. His mind went blank from fear and overload and then he heard a voice in his head saying "trust the force Luke." The voice was telling him to trust himself, to trust his instincts, to not think about it…just do it.

That's what you need to do. Trust yourself, trust your instincts, let it go and let your SubCom handle it.

**Trust the force!**

# I DECLARE

*"The ordinary acts we practice every day at home, are of more importance to the soul than their simplicity might suggest."*

Thomas Moore

## Subconscious Mind Hack# 2: Daily Declarations

Daily declarations are the key to unlocking The Law. They're to the mind, what exercise is to the body. I've said before that we're shaped by our thoughts…that we always believe what we tell ourselves. Well, just as if you constantly emphasize a limiting belief you start to believe it, the same holds true for positive statements. This is when believing what you say to yourself is a good thing. You can achieve everything you want if you believe in yourself and build a positive mindset. You do that with daily declarations.

## What Are Daily Declarations?

You're probably more familiar with the word affirmations. It's the same thing just different wording. Daily declarations or affirmations are empowering mantra's that have profound effects on the conscious and subconscious. Simply put, it's speaking your goals into truth. Rapper Jay-Z is a believer. He's been quoted as saying he believes you can speak things into existence.

When Joe first wrote about this it was revolutionary. No one really understood the power of affirmations as we do today, though the concept has been around since biblical days. The bible says to "take every thought captive." (2 Corinthians 10:5). That's what this is…taking control of our thoughts to use the power of positive self-talk to drown out the negative thoughts.

The singer Lizzo has her own daily mantra and has actually led her audience into saying it at her concerts; "I love you. You are beautiful and you can do anything." I love that she does that not only for herself but that she introduces affirmations to hundreds of thousands of others. Words are powerful.

Many sports figures and celebrities use affirmations. They've succeeded because of the positive mindset they've built that they're constantly reinforcing with affirmations. They become disciplined, focused, "driven" and winners in whatever area they put that focus in. For example, do you remember what self-declaration the great boxer Muhammad Ali was

> IT'S SPEAKING YOUR GOALS INTO TRUTH.

known for? He was constantly saying, "I am the Greatest" to himself and any cameras in front of him. Just oozing self-confidence and belief in himself and his abilities.

He later said in an interview that he started saying that *even before he knew* he was that good. He was **speaking it into truth.** He explained affirmations this way; "It's the *repetition* of affirmations that leads to belief. And once that belief becomes a deep conviction, things begin to happen."

## It's A Mind Shift

Whether you know it or not, you're already using daily declarations but it's usually not so positive. Remember I talked about self-bullying? Think about what comes out of your mouth to yourself throughout the day. "That's just the way I am and I can't change now," or "I know I'm not good enough for that new job."

We don't even realize we're doing it, but those negative thoughts and self-talk are constantly reinforcing your limiting beliefs. **You're self-bullying and no one can thrive under that verbal abuse.** No Woo Woo stuff here. Just common sense about unfortunate common behavior.

The daily declaration process is about letting go of those negative thoughts that fill your head and come out of your mouth and replacing it with positive thoughts to come out of your mouth instead. **It's to build your belief as the foundation for who you want to become.**

Your daily declaration is a positive statement of belief, even though when you begin working with a declaration you may not believe it. If you already believed, you wouldn't have to work to develop it, right? Just remember, even the "greatest" Muhammad Ali didn't believe he was the greatest when he first started saying it, but he kept repeating it until he and the world *did* believe it.

By constantly repeating that statement, you're planting that positive message in your subconscious, and there it will begin to overcome your previous training, mindsets, and beliefs that reinforced all that negativity.

As a young girl, Oprah had a daily declaration growing up that she created after watching her grandmother work so hard. She said to herself over and over again, "My life won't be like this. My life won't be like this, it will be better." Those daily declarations seemed to do the trick for her. Just sayin'.

## Plant the Right Seeds

Think of your subconscious as a garden where all kinds of random seeds have taken root. There might be a lot of beneficial plants there, but there will also be a lot of weeds. Negative limiting attitudes are like weeds. They have deep roots and multiply rapidly, taking over everything and ruining the garden.

The daily declaration process is just a way of planting the right kinds of seeds and planting them in such large quantities that they eventually overwhelm the weeds and slowly replace them with confidence building productive and helpful attitudes.

## Own It

After a breakup, my best friend made an actual t-shirt of her self-declaration to remind herself that it was the other persons loss, because she's all that and a bag of chips.

Her t shirt simply said; "Yes, I am…."

As you can imagine, when she wore it out, everyone asked "Yes I am…. what?"

The answer to that question depended on what she was feeling that day… "Yes I am a strong powerful black woman," or "Yes I am worthy of finding the right person that appreciates me for who I am." Whatever the answer, it was empowering and a constant positive reinforcement…a daily declaration.

The secret to daily declarations is that **you need to feel the emotion** of the statements, not repeat them in some robotic manner because I told you to. Remember, this is your life, not homework. The whole point is that they are to provide inspiration to your mind, body and soul. Make a t-shirt with your declaration like she did. Own it!

## Show Me The Money...

Visualization is an active and important part of daily declarations. It uses the imagination as a tool to create success or build certain personality qualities we need to achieve our goals, because remember…the Universe will provide what we hold in our minds.

Phil Jackson was a former NBA coach of the Chicago Bulls and LA Lakers and one of the personalities profiled on Netflix documentary "The Last Dance." He said in his book *Sacred Hoops* that he used to invite all of his players into a meditation circle before every important playoff game to envision the outcome of them winning the game. In case you didn't know, they won a lot.

Skier Lindsey Vonn is one of the most successful skiers in history and a Gold Medalist. Before she retired, she said she always visualized the run before she did it. "By the time I get to the start gate, I've run that race 100 times already in my head."

> THE SECRET TO DAILY DECLARATIONS IS THAT YOU NEED TO FEEL THE EMOTION OF THE STATEMENTS.

Here's how Arnold Schwarzenegger used visualization as a tool for his success;

> "When I was very young, I visualized myself being and having what I wanted. I never had doubts. The mind is so incredible. Before I won my first Mr. Universe title, I walked around the tournament like I owned it. The title was already mine in my head. I had won it so many times in my mind that there was no doubt I would win it. Then when I moved on to the movies, the same thing. I visualized myself being a famous actor and earning big money. I could feel and taste success. I just knew it would all happen."

And it did.

You may not be coaching a NBA team, doing a ski run for an Olympic medal, or going for the Mr. Universe title, but visualization is key for no matter what goal you're going for. Oprah made creating Vision Boards popular years ago. Those are a great tool for visualizing what it is you want to manifest. I highly recommend making one of those to be the ultimate visualization.

"YOU'RE SAYING WHAT FEELS LIKE A LIE, BUT THEN ONE DAY THE LIE IS TRUE."

## Now Its Your Turn

So now that you have an understanding of the daily declaration and how it plays a role in your intentional shift, it's time to create your own. Here's an example of a daily declaration; "I am free of all past limiting attitudes and am confident in my abilities."

When creating your own daily declaration, keep these in mind.

### State it as if it's already true.
Say "I am…" or " I have…"

### Focus on the result you want to achieve, not on what you are trying to eliminate.
Say "I am confident" …not… "I am not nervous." Learn to focus on the positive.

### Use strong, vivid words that will capture your imagination.
Luxurious… beachfront home where I hear the waves crashing right outside my door and smell the fresh ocean air.

### Be specific!
State exactly the result you want to achieve. Get in the habit of asking for what you want.

### Work on yourself.
Don't make declarations about others because you can't really change them, or their attitudes. The secret to changing other people's attitudes is to change your own, and by seeing your example that may inspire them to change themselves.

Richard always said; "You live your life one of two ways; either you live your life as an example…or you live your life as a warning." Make your life an example to follow. When others see the change in you, they will want to follow you!

## Remember…They're DAILY Declarations
Make them a part of your daily routine.

Author Jack Canfield says "Repeating an affirmation several times a day keeps you focused on your goal, strengthens your motivation, and programs your subconscious by sending an order to your crew to do whatever it takes to make it happen."

Jennifer Lopez has said her day is incomplete without at least 15 minutes dedicated to affirmations. Seems to have worked for her and many others, so why not?

Let me leave you with this last one.

Superstar singer Lady Gaga had a specific daily declaration she repeated to herself religiously every day before she was a superstar. "Music is my life. Music is my life. The fame is inside of me. I'm going to make a number one record and the number one hit."

She said it felt like you're "Telling yourself a lie because it hadn't happened yet. You're saying what feels like a lie over and over again…but then one day, the lie is true!"

Her "lie" certainly came true. Point made. Boom. Drop the mic!

## Now go forth and declare!

# CHAPTER 11
# A SUPER SUGGESTION

*"When you are willing to stop looking for something in thought,
You find everything in silence."*

Gangaji

## Subconscious Mind Hack # 3: Super Suggestion

There's a saying that the goal of meditation isn't to control your thoughts, it's to stop letting them control you. As you've learned by now, the underlying principle of this book is to guide you through a mind shift to take control of your thoughts and to stop letting them control you. This mindhack is another tool to use to take control.

In Chapter Nine, you learned about the ultimate mind hack…discovering your subconscious computer, and now you've learned two of the other subconscious mind hacks used with that discovery, Daily Declarations and your Grown-Up Time Out.

With your Grown-Up Time Out, you're learning how to be silent and have a peaceful pause in your day to refresh your mind.

With your Daily Declarations, you're verbally affirming what you want. Your empowering mantras are used for either tangible or intangible things on your lists that you're speaking into truth.

Super Suggestion is the last of the subconscious mind hacks. This one is used to **build yourself up**. All energy goes to building the intangible personal qualities you want to build up in yourself; positive attitudes, empowering beliefs, confidence and enhancing self-talk, among others.

It's a technique designed to relax your mind, body and emotions and drown out the external, and more importantly *internal* "noise" that clutters our mind daily. In our completely conscious state we "edit" the information we feed our brain; talking ourselves out of what we really want, for whatever the reason we give ourselves, or other people decide for us. We mind f**k ourselves right out of it.

As you've learned, the subconscious believes everything you tell it. This daily discipline teaches you to take the time to breathe and get in a relaxed state enough to unlock your subconscious and be open to the suggestions you feed it…the Super Suggestion! Your Super Suggestion creates full belief even before the personality goal has been achieved.

SUPER SUGGESTION IS USED TO BUILD YOURSELF UP.

Unlike daily declarations where we say them loud and proud wherever you can find uninterrupted space...with this you find a quiet dimly lit space to reach a more relaxed state where you can focus only on you and planting the super suggestion in your subconscious.

## WWJD?

This concept that Joe first introduced many years ago, is based on ancient knowledge. In the Bible, Jesus taught his disciples the same technique as a way to pray; and it's found in the fundamental teachings of many other religions, but it wasn't widely practiced in Joe's day. It was considered *new age,* as were affirmations, supposedly used at that time by only the stereotypical new age followers, the "crunchy tree-hugger types."

But people know better now, and it's accepted worldwide including in the field of psychology, because it has been studied, dissected and proven to work.

## Log Off

Super Suggestion is basically a form of meditation... but to do it, you don't need to be in the lotus pose with chanting and incense...unless that's your thing. I mean it wouldn't hurt. You just need to find 20 minutes in a quiet space. A place to "let go." Be sure your phone is on mute so it's not blowing up with news alert tweets and Tik Tok videos while you're getting in the relaxed state you'll need to be in for this hack to be effective.

Dr. Joseph Murray says, "You can build radiant health, success and happiness by the thoughts you think in the hidden studio of your mind." So once a day, for just 15-20 minutes, take the time to go to the hidden studio in your mind and repeat the qualities you're building in yourself with wording as if already achieved, like you do with your daily declarations. Like... "I am capable and confident."

Robert Baden-Powell says..."A man carries out suggestions more wholeheartedly when he understands their aim." Let me explain why it works, so you can carry out the suggestion more wholeheartedly.

## Suggestion Acceptance Or Rejection

We all have different levels of consciousness that we experience at one time of the day or another. That's anywhere from 100% awake and aware… to maybe 45% where you're kind of half asleep, like after lunch… to 0% which means you're in the hospital. When you're in a deep sleep, you're still about 10% conscious.

With that in mind think about how you'd react to *suggestions* from a source outside your own body in different levels of consciousness. To explain what I mean, I'll use an athlete as example.

Say you have a pro sports champion, intent and alert. He hears screaming and shouts directed to him from all over the stadium. No problem. He's a trained professional. His own mind is in full control of his consciousness and doesn't need to take *suggestions* from spectators in the crowd.

But, you take that same athlete, awakened from a sound drooling sleep, still drowsy, and he might be fooled into running for an exit with the false suggestion, "GET OUT OF HERE, THE ROOM'S ON FIRE!" Every muscle of his body would then be reacting, *not to his own conscious mind,* but to the suggestion!

These two examples; suggestion *rejection* on the playing field… and suggestion *acceptance* in the half-awake state, explain how Super Suggestion works. In both cases the same mind received the outside suggestion, right? The only differences were the *condition of consciousness* at the moment of suggestion creating the *power of the suggestion.*

In the suggestion *rejection* case, he had a fully conscious, concentrated mind and he paid attention to it. However, in the *accepted* suggestion situation, his conscious level was compromised, so the conscious mind didn't have time to filter, making him more open to the suggestion.

That level of consciousness is what makes all the difference, and is the concept behind this whole subconscious mind hack. The conscious mind filters…blocking "suggestions" fed to it. The subconscious mind is more relaxed, doesn't filter and therefore is more open to the "suggestions" fed to it.

Let me just say I've learned from other readers that in the beginning, that just like the Grown Up Time Out, it was hard for them to find the 20 minutes a day to do this. But once they made it a priority and found the time, they looked forward to it every day and became more confident each day because of taking control of their mind. You will too.

Day by day, as you perform these three easy peasy subconscious mind hacks, your subconscious computer enhances every decision, making you unstoppable…the boss of you!

So…now that you're armed with theses tools to help you be unstoppable, let's discuss the things that up until now…may have been stopping you. This is where the real talk begins, because by being aware and working through them, you're moving them out of your way permanently.

Let's get to it boss.

# CHAPTER 12
# WHO'S THE BOSS?

> *"The greatest discovery of my generation
> is that a human being can alter his life
> by altering his attitudes of mind."*
>
> William James

## Daybeak

*There's a peaceful silence out here broken only by the sound of a dog drinking from the lake.*

*The suns brightness lights up the sky so that we can see all of God's beauty around us;*

*The clouds reflections on the still water as the birds fly over it, chirping*

> *The design the water makes in the sand during the night,*
>
> *And the winds calming breeze in the morning air.*
>
> *Now and then I'll see a turtle's head pop out above the water upsetting the calmness of the lake*
>
> *And it reminds me of my life; calm and peaceful until something comes along to upset it all*
>
> *But tomorrow morning it will be calm and peaceful again.*

I wrote this poem one early morning when I was 15 years old sitting on the dock of our lake house. A poet I'm not, but I needed to get my feelings out on paper that day and this is what came out.

I was there with my dad, his new wife and their new baby girl. I was a daddy's girl and until then had not only been the baby of the family, but the only girl. I was going through all the emotions you would expect I'd be going through. My small teenage world had been turned upside down.

My original ending wasn't that last line; "But tomorrow morning it will be calm and peaceful again."

It ended with the turtle upsetting the calmness of the water, which in my 15-year-old mind was a metaphor for the new wife and new baby that came and upset the calmness of my *life*.

I walked back up from the dock to the lake house and at their request read the poem to my dad and stepmom. True to my stepmom's ever-present positive attitude, she said "But you know tomorrow it will be calm and peaceful again. That's how life is."

We never discussed the *real* meaning of the poem, but I thought about it the rest of the day and decided maybe she was right. My life would be ok, it would be calm and peaceful again in my new normal, so I got over myself and added her words as a positive ending to the poem.

> IT WAS A SIMPLE MIND SHIFT AND IT CHANGED ME FOREVER.

I don't know what was different that day and why my mind was open, but it was a simple mind shift and it changed me forever. I grew up that day and my world got much larger…the day I became boss of my attitude and chose to embrace my new family…the day I learned that a change of attitude can change your life.

## Don't Be An Eeyore

One of the greatest gifts you possess as a human is your attitude. You own it. You control it. You're 100% responsible for it. You're the only one who can change it. **You're the boss of it!**

If you have a bad day for whatever reason, I get it. Sometimes other people frustrate us and it affects our mood. Sometimes we frustrate ourselves and it affects our mood. It's those days when happiness, for whatever reason requires too much energy, so its ok to gripe and bitch. I, too, have days like that where I don't even want to be around *myself*. We're human and it's understandable every once in a while.

But some people live their **whole lives** with a bad attitude. They let themselves stay consistently miserable, making them miserable to be around. Know anyone like that? They gripe and bitch about everyone and everything, and hold on to baggage, making sure everyone knows about it. I call them Eeyore's…you know the depressing AF donkey in *Winnie the Pooh*…because they're so depressing and draining. Don't be an Eeyore.

No one wants to be around an Eeyore. As Dolly Parton says, "You gotta work hard at being happy just like some folks work hard at being miserable."

## The Pike Syndrome

Many people hold onto baggage and let it keep them miserable. Baggage is such a huge topic you'll hear it mentioned throughout the book and I have a full chapter on it later. But for purposes of this chapter, we'll discuss one of the biggest pieces of baggage; the attitude with limiting beliefs that leads to learned helplessness. Let me explain with a true story. A story about a fish. Yep…a fish.

There's a short documentary about an experiment originally done more than a century ago by German zoologist Dr. Karl Mobus about *learned helplessness*. It's impact is so powerful it has a clinical name; The Pike Syndrome. Google it. It's on YouTube.

The experimental study begins with a psychologist putting a Northern Pike in a large aquarium. A Northern Pike is a large strong fish that feeds on smaller fish and it's favorite dish is minnows. When the psychologist put minnows in the aquarium, the pike would just chow down on every minnow put in the tank.

After watching and learning how the pike feeds, the psychologist then placed clear glass cylinders in the aquarium and put the minnows *inside* the cylinders. When the pike tries to feed now, he doesn't know the glass cylinders have been put there, he can't see them, so he does what he does and tries to eat the minnows like he did so easily before.

But now every time he tries to take a minnow…Bam! He gets a very painful bop on the nose. You can see him shake it off, then try again. And again…Bam! Another bop on the nose. He tries again. Bam. Bam. Bam. Bam. Well, that would hurt after a while, even to a fish, so he stops trying. He's learned through the pain that no matter how tempting, no matter how hungry he gets, he just can't have the minnows anymore. Not only can he not have them, it's painful to even try to get them.

When the psychologist is satisfied that the Pike has stopped trying, he removes the glass cylinders releasing the minnows to swim freely. The minnows are now swimming all around the Pike, but he makes absolutely no moves to try and get one. His favorite food is surrounding him, and he won't move a muscle to get it, because he's learned it hurts to try to get something he thinks he can't have. **He will literally starve to death in the midst of abundance because he has formed the limiting belief that he can't have it!**

This is the Pike Syndrome. This is **learned helplessness.**

# Hardening Of The Attitudes

Unfortunately, we're all capable of falling victim to learned helplessness. We sit and "starve", hungering for wealth, or love and respect, and it's all within easy reach. But we're surrounded by layers of glass walls that we put up or let others put up around us. Trying and failing several times leaves us feeling that we have no control, so, like the Pike, we stop trying. We won't risk getting bopped on the nose by hitting the glass to get what we want. We've quit before we've even tried. We've learned to be helpless.

But here's the thing. You can *choose to* not be a victim of your attitudes, beliefs, baggage, or life situation. You have the power to change your situation and your belief system set up by yourself and others by changing your attitude. It's as easy as it sounds and yet…it's not always so easy.

As Master Motivator Zig Ziglar said, "Hardening of the *attitudes* is more common than hardening of the arteries." Sometimes it takes others to help… mentors, therapists, coaches and lifechanging personal growth books like this to push us beyond our comfort zone, out of the limiting belief boundaries, to lasting change.

You're learning that an essential part of your life, is that you **take control of your own mind, otherwise you'll just stay stuck in your smallness in the midst of abundance.**

Victor Frankl author of the classic book *Man's Search for Meaning*, was a prominent German Psychiatrist who survived the holocaust in Auschwitz. This is what *he* said about attitude.

"The last great freedom of man is the freedom to choose his attitude under any given circumstances. You can't control what happens to you, but you *can* control your *attitude* towards what happens to you, and in that, you will be **mastering change rather than allowing it to master you**."

Mastering his attitude is what helped him survive the horrors of Auschwitz. If he can do it for *that*, you can do it for your life.

## "Have To's" vs "Choose To's"

One way to take control of your mind is to change your attitude about how you look at things you feel you "have to" do. It's a simple shift in wording and attitude, but with life changing results.

When you think you *have to* do something, you aren't motivated because it makes you feel like someone else is making you do it. Who likes that? ***Choosing to* do it gives the power back to you** and all is well with the world.

I'm using this concept successfully for weight loss, which I'll discuss in the chapter on habits. But let me tell you about a woman I read about who was sick and tired of all the things she felt she had to do… all the "adulting" in her life that seemed to be for everyone but her.

> "CHOOSING" TO DO IT GIVES THE POWER BACK TO YOU.

She calculated where she was spending her energy, her self-imposed "have tos" and realized she wasn't getting much happiness. As a matter of fact, others were reaping the happiness at her expense. So, she decided to give herself a happiness raise and give herself more of the things she wanted but had been denying, including time for herself.

To do this, she instituted a new rule; anytime she felt she *should* do or *had* to do something, she took the time to evaluate it before committing. Did she really *have to* attend a baby shower when she would rather have a self-care day? She learned to respectfully say no to some things and found the world not only didn't end, her world got hella better. She stopped wasting energy on things she didn't want to do and could say no to, and suddenly she had the clarity and bandwidth for all the things she used to say she didn't have time for.

Remember I talked about where to find time for a Grown-Up Time Out or Super Suggestion? Here's a way to get some…and be happier. Score!

## Be A Bueller…A "Why Not?"

Have you ever seen the classic movie "Ferris Bueller's Day Off?" Here's a guy who never felt the need to *have to* do anything he didn't want to do. He gave himself a happiness raise every single day. Bueller was a high school student and a slacker for sure. I'm definitely not advocating that part of his character. What I *do* love about his character is his zest for life. He went after and did everything he wanted, with a positive attitude. Nothing holds him back including that little thing called going to class. He didn't have fears or limiting beliefs or worry about what others thought of him blocking him from living his best life. He had a "Why Not?" attitude.

Let me explain that concept. I've discovered through my years that most people seem to have either a "Why?" or a "Why not?" attitude about life.

For example, I'll suggest to my friend that we go on a spontaneous road trip. She immediately responds with "Why?" I respond back just as quickly with "Why Not?" Think about it. Are you a "Why?" or a "Why Not?"

Life's choices often come down to a decision between those two questions. My personal belief is the "Whys?" of our life may not necessarily be an Eeyore, but they hold themselves back from so much of what life has to offer.

I came out of the womb with a "Why Not?" attitude, as did my husband. Our "Why Nots?" led us on many great adventures together all over the world. Point is, why not…be a "Why Not?" (See what I did there?) Life is too short to fret over so many "Whys?" and let them hold you back from living your Best Life. Just be a responsible one.

## You Are Response-Able

Here's the main point, you are the boss of you and your attitudes! You are ultimately response-**able** for controlling your attitudes and you have the ability to control your responses to any situation. You can't change the events of your past, and you may or may not be able to change your current circumstances immediately, however, you *can* change your attitudes about those things. The attitudes are not carved in stone, so just change those that don't work for you with the help of your subconscious computer.

The subconscious does only what it's told and you're in control of what instructions the subconscious receives. You've been learning to take control of programming your subconscious. Use those tools available to you to make the changes to your attitude too. Make it one of your daily declarations.

Choose to be the boss of your attitudes! Yes, it really is that easy. When you do, you can do anything you want with your future. I'm so glad I learned to be the boss of my attitude so early in life. It changed my world, because remember…like attracts like. I surrounded myself with positive people which manifested positive, exciting life experiences. A life of "Why nots?"

So, get to it Bueller. **Get an Attitude Adjustment.**

Bueller, Bueller?

(See the movie and you'll get it.)

# BE THE CHANGE

*"You will either step forward into growth, or you will step back into safety."*

Abraham Maslow

*It is never too late,*

*or in my case too early*

*to be whoever you want to be.*

*There's no time limit.*

*Start whenever you want.*

*You can change or stay the same.*

*There are no rules to this thing.*

*We can make the best or the worst of it.*

*I hope you make the best of it.*

*I hope you see things that startle you.*

*I hope you feel things you never felt before.*

*I hope you meet people who have a different point of view.*

*I hope you live a life you're proud of*

*And if you're not*

*I hope you have the courage to start all over again.*

F. Scott Fitzgerald and used in the Screenplay of *"The Curious Case of Benjamin Button"*

## Real Talk

So, how are you doing so far?
**Are you feeling things you never felt before?**
I bet you are.

**Are you making the best of it?**
Are you reading with intention?

**Do you have the courage to be whoever you want to be?**
Are you still with me or are your limiting beliefs rearing their ugly head?

I'm doing a check in because I realize I've given you a lot to process so far. New and different things that challenge you to go way beyond your comfort zone; to *think only of yourself* and not others for a change, to self-evaluate, make changes, perform new routines and adopt a new attitude. That's a lot. It takes courage to start again.

For most of you, I know you've got this. You're feeling strong and empowered making these changes and are right on track. For the others that may be overwhelmed and thinking it's just too much, I get it. I know some of you are fighting it, getting bogged down by your life in the minute, your present, and are thinking of giving up your future better life. I want to address it here and now so you rethink it and move forward confidently.

## This S**T's Real

The reason you may be starting to feel overwhelmed is because it's becoming real. You're realizing that to have a better life you're going to need to actually take action and make some changes, *not just talk about it*. And, because of the action you've already taken, you're also starting to *see change,* which is great of course, but can be uncomfortable even when it's a good change so you might be feeling some kind of way about that. That's normal.

But what most often gets in the way at this point, is that the people in your life are starting to see changes in you too and the toxic ones have started pushing your "limiting beliefs" button to cause doubt and to try and hold you back. You're growing, and they aren't. They're jealous and you're afraid of losing them so you stop working on achieving your Best Life, for them.

I can't tell you how many people I've worked with through the years that let the fear of outgrowing their spouse or significant others smallness**,** stop them from continuing the progress already made and kept them sitting in their discomfort.

It's normal to *feel* those feels, but don't let it stop you, or nothing will ever change. They won't respect you. As a matter of fact, they'll use it against you to make themselves feel bigger, with an "I told you so." Then you won't respect yourself, and you're back to square one. Don't get caught in that dead-end cycle. Spirit, a therapist on Oprah's Network "OWN" said it poetically…**"don't set yourself on fire to keep someone else warm."**

## Don't Let Your Light Be Dimmed

I'm sure you've heard the phrase; "We become a part of who we're around." Truth! The people in your tribe have a legit impact on your attitudes and what kind of life you live.

Whitney Houston in an interview with Oprah once described how her relationship with husband Bobby Brown "dimmed her light." She was the superstar but let herself get trapped in her husband's smallness, which affected her life, habits, health and career…ultimately causing the premature end of her life.

Don't let someone in *your* life dim your light. This is the new grown ass you! If your friends, family, or significant other don't support you, then they're showing you that they don't want the best for you. Who wants people that don't want the best for you in their life?

Remember in Chapter Seven I talked about letting go of toxic people? For those toxic people who may be rearing their ugly heads, just say "Bye Felicia" and let them know**… "I'm making some changes in my life. If you don't hear from me, you're one of them"**…and move them out of your life. Find new people who want to help you shine brighter. You deserve it.

> DON'T LET SOMEONE ELSE'S SMALLNESS LEAVE YOU SITTING IN YOUR DISCOMFORT.

So, what can also happen at this point, is you start pushing *your own* limiting beliefs button. Your glass walls…fear of change, limiting beliefs, limiting *people*, and unpacked baggage, seem to get bigger in your mind. You're facing them head on, which becomes overwhelming and you create all kinds of excuses on why you can't continue. Some people decide they've changed *just enough* to escape their immediate problems, but it's a Band-Aid when surgery is actually needed.

## Get An Attitude Adjustment

You've heard the saying…Insanity is doing the same thing over and over and expecting a different result? That brings us back to being the boss of your attitude. Stop the insanity. **You're the only one with the power** to do it!

It's time to stop trying to *only* solve your problems, *only* react to your current circumstances instead of being proactive and *it's time to stop listening* to the people in your life trying to get in your business. To make true change, to level up from where you are to where you want to be, you'll need to think bigger. You'll need an attitude adjustment.

With a shift in attitude, you realize change is powerful, exciting and can take you to new places and positive people. When I shifted my attitude back at age 15, my whole world opened up. Remember…like attracts like. I was more positive which attracted more positive people and my life snowballed from good to amazing! It was like in the movie "The Wizard of Oz" when it went from black and white to color.

## Who Created Your Glass Walls?

You're not entirely responsible for the walls being put there in the first place any more than the Pike was responsible for putting the glass wall between himself and the minnows. There are thousands of events in everyone's life that can result in glass walls.

Without realizing it, we're open to the suggestions of others, leading to walls being built by friends, family, church leaders and teachers. People who laugh at you when you express your dreams. People who, out of love, warn you not to get your hopes too high so you won't be disappointed. Verbal abuse that you take as gospel and hold onto, or beliefs and attitudes leftover from Generational Trauma. And one by one your glass walls go up.

## Take Off Your Mask

Or you're living with someone else's belief system. We take on an identity with our parents which is natural as we're growing up, but we hold onto it for way too long. There comes a time when you become an adult and should start making your own choices and forming your own independent belief system.

We take on an identity with our significant other as well, and so often get stuck in that identity for the lifetime of the relationship. Understandably, if one person continues to grow and the other doesn't, that often leads to an unhappy relationship.

Actors Will Smith and his life partner Jada Pinkett Smith had a discussion about this on her outstanding Facebook Watch Web TV series, "Red Table Talk". Will thought everything was cool with their relationship because they were successful and had all the "things." Jada said she wasn't happy and felt she wasn't living her authentic self anymore. Ends up they were both just trying to live up to an idea of each other, feeling the stress of the obligations and expectations… "feeling trapped by their vows." Damn, now that's some real talk.

They described that what can happen in a long-term relationship, is the person you're with ends up loving your "mask" that's put on over time and so it stays on. But to get real and grow, you need to take off the mask, start breaking down the fantasies of relationships that start at a young age and take time for yourself to be two separate people who can grow as they live life together. They took that time off to grow as separate humans and were able to grow back together for an even stronger, more fulfilling authentic relationship.

## Do You Boo

Maybe you live with a cultural belief system or societal stereotype. Many seem to feel the need to fit into certain roles that they're born into dictated by family, ethnicity, religious beliefs, societal pressures, economics and heritage. But maybe your cultural belief system is not you, you've been living it out of fear, or loyalty and respect for your family...whatever family means to you.

Again though...one life to live. If the life you're living is one where you have to wear a "mask" in your love life or any part of your life, commit your life to someone else's religious or cultural beliefs, or any other stereotype you've accepted for yourself and, here's the important part... *it isn't working for you...* then now is the time for you to stop living that other life. If they do work for you, Mazeltov, it's a match. All I'm saying is you can only be truly authentically happy living your own life. Your own beliefs. Your truth. Do you Boo.

## Its Your Choice

There are so many people and experiences that have helped mold you into the person you are today. And while you may not be the one who put those walls there in the first place, you are definitely the one who *keeps* them there. The only thing that's in your way is you. The old you; the old habits and the old attitudes; past experiences, obstacles and roadblocks from yesterday that are still locked in your mind. Don't waste time looking back, holding on to things and people holding you back. Life's too short.

My life coach gives this sobering advice... "Stop holding yourself or others accountable for something that happened years ago. If you keep drudging it up and talking about it, it stays alive. It's like digging up a grave." In other words, let shit from the past go and focus on what you've learned since then, and move on!

Are your burning desires just "Wouldn't it be nice if's?"

No? They *really are* your burning desires? Ok then. When you want something you've never had, you have to do something you've never done. So, you my friend are at a turning point…you have a choice.

You can go back to just talking about it and stay stuck *or* take action and keep moving forward. You can let others dim your light for you, or you can make a better life for yourself without them. You can sit around and blame your parents, teachers, cultural traditions, and the other people who helped build your glass walls and stay stuck right where you are…or you can let go of the past, tear down the glass walls, continue doing you and get on to living your best life by continuing to read this book with intention.

You get to be in control of the changes. You're learning the tools to remove the roadblocks that have been sitting there for years or maybe all your life. Don't let it go to waste just because you or someone in your life is *temporarily* uncomfortable.

## Live A Life You're Proud Of

Sit down and have a real talk with yourself.

You're the only one who can decide who you want to become, what you'll be happy doing the rest of your life and who you want to share it with. You're in charge of you. So, don't stop your flow. Keep working on you. Don't let others stop you from "doing you."

> Remember…
> It is never too late,
>  to be whoever you want to be.
> You can change or stay the same…
> …I hope you live a life you're proud of
> And if you're not
> I hope you have the courage to start all over again.

Your mission…should you choose to accept it…is to have the courage to continue so you can live a life you're proud of. So, take a deep breath, remember why you chose this book and let's move forward.

# YOU'VE BEEN HYPNOTIZED

*"We are all in a post-hypnotic trance induced in early infancy."*

R.D.Laing

We talked about change in the last chapter and how important it is in moving forward. I'm sure I wasn't telling you anything you didn't already know. So why do we as humans, knowing we need to make certain changes…don't? Well here's something you may *not* know; the reason change can be so difficult is we've been hypnotized. Let me explain.

## Post-Hypnotic Suggestion

Have you ever done something, realized you shouldn't have done it, decided you'd never do it again, and then turned right around and repeated the same behavior or action again, and again? Of course, you have. We all have. It stems from Post-Hypnotic Suggestions.

Simply put, Post-Hypnotic Suggestion is a tool used by hypnotherapists to stimulate their clients into correcting whatever behavior they want corrected. Say, the client wants to quit smoking. The Post-Hypnotic suggestion is a suggestion the therapist recommends to the client under hypnosis for them to subconsciously remember after the session. Such as, the suggestion that *cigarettes taste terrible and make everything reek of smoke*, theoretically stopping the client from wanting a cigarette after hypnosis.

## The British Are Coming

The Post-Hypnotic Suggestion became known to those *not* in hypnotherapy by a famous hypnotist back in the day named Pat Collins. She was known as the "Hip Hypnotist" and became popular with the celebrities of that time, even hypnotizing comedian Lucille Ball on an episode of her show.

For years she owned a popular nightclub in LA where she performed her hypnosis on the audience members. During the show, she would suggest certain situations to her hypnotized volunteers, like… 'laugh out loud at the funny movie you're seeing in your mind.' And as soon as she gave the suggestion to the hypnotized group she had up on stage, they'd all immediately behave as if they were *really* watching a funny movie and would start to laugh hysterically.

After having fun with that for a while, she then demonstrated her post-hypnotic suggestion. Before taking them out of the trance, she would give one last outrageous suggestion for them to do once they were out from under the hypnotic state… **a post-hypnotic suggestion**. She told her volunteers that after they came out from under hypnosis, they would jump up and start shouting "The British are coming! The British are coming!" each time she mentioned the name of her club.

She then brought them out of their trance and told them to go back to their seats in the audience. As they were sitting back down, she thanked them for helping her with her act at the "Pat Collins Celebrity Club." Immediately they started acting out the post-hypnotic suggestion by jumping up hollering "The British are coming! The British are coming!" It was now the *never* hypnotized audience members who were laughing hysterically. You can see it on YouTube. Check it out.

When interviewed later, the volunteers said *they were aware* that what they were saying or doing wasn't their conscious choice, and they even told themselves they wouldn't react to her outrageous suggestion, and yet they did every time!

Well, that's what happens to us. Remember that thing we keep doing over and over again though we tell ourselves we won't? At some point in our life, we were given a post-hypnotic suggestion that we aren't even aware of, just like the hypnotized group wasn't aware they'd been given a "suggestion" to shout out "the British are coming."

## You've Been Hypnotized

Yes, somewhere along the way, we've been "hypnotized." Not in the theatrical sense of the word of course, but in a more damaging, longer lasting way.

You've accepted certain "suggestions" about yourself and your behavior from outside influences; your parents, teacher, your siblings, your boss, or your spouse…someone whose opinion you valued enough to take to heart and create this suggestive pattern in your mind that has blocked your progress up to this point.

Much of it happened when you were just a child. A lot of your limiting programming came from your lack of understanding of the world around you and the natural inclination of children to look up to and accept what bigger children and adults tell them. You *accepted* all kinds of suggestions about yourself and the world around you.

Whether as a child with your parents or a teacher, or as an adult with a boss or a spouse, the post-hypnotic suggestions are partly responsible for creating the glass walls you have up and the mask you wear, as we discussed in the last chapter.

I know it might be hard to believe that it could've happened to you, but it's very natural to go in and out of a hypnotic state many times a day. Think about it. We make a million little decisions each day without even thinking. Our brains are too busy, so we perform routine things throughout the day like taking showers, washing dishes, or getting dressed…all on auto pilot. Or like I've mentioned previously, sometimes driving to work, getting there without having any thought of how you got there.

So, doesn't it sound feasible that we've let situations, or other's "suggestions" or words affect us without really knowing it, creating post-hypnotic suggestions?

## Triggers

The post-hypnotic suggestion needs a cue, or a trigger to be uh, triggered. It can be anything from a specific time or place, to an event, a smell, or simply a few words.

The trigger brings you back subconsciously to the time when the suggestion was originally unknowingly enforced, and off you go shouting, "The British are coming! The British are coming!" Not for real of course. It's more subtle than that, but the concept is the same… we're under "hypnosis" and we carry it out without consciously thinking about it.

> THE FIRST PART OF BREAKING THE PATTERN IS TO BECOME AWARE OF THE ROADBLOCK YOU DIDN'T EVEN KNOW EXISTED.

Often the trigger is a certain kind of situation or environment. For example, let's say you have a great idea for doing an aspect of your job more effectively. If you can sell your employer on the idea, it'll probably mean a promotion and a raise; but each time you try to approach the boss with the idea you become nervous and tongue-tied. You begin to doubt yourself and your idea and end up blowing it. Your whole presentation is a hot mess. A couple weeks later, one of your co-workers steals your idea, takes it to the boss and sells it. He gets the credit and the raise, and your post-hypnotic suggestion is reinforced all over again. Problem is you don't know that's what it is because it's embedded in your subconscious. You're left feeling defeated once again and wonder why you can't seem to communicate effectively with the boss. It just keeps the vicious cycle going and your self-confidence getting beaten up.

Well, now you know. Sometime in your past you accepted the "suggestion" that you don't do well talking to authority figures. Maybe it was a bad school experience with a teacher, or principle, or maybe it was a problem speaking to an intimidating parent.

You can't really go back and change the kind of programming you received as a child. So, does that mean you're stuck with who you are? Absolutely not. The first part of breaking the pattern is to become aware of the roadblock you didn't even know existed. My goal with this chapter was to introduce you to the fact that you've been dealing with this previously unknown to you concept of post-hypnotic suggestions. Now we can work on un-hypnotizing you, but I also recommend speaking to a professional to work through it if it's too big to handle alone.

## Become Un-Hypnotized

Before Pat finished her hypnosis act, she was careful to remove all post-hypnotic suggestions. After all, it could be embarrassing to suddenly jump up and shout, "The British are coming" at a dinner party just because someone happened to mention the Pat Collins Celebrity Club.

But suppose one night she had forgotten? It would have been okay because **Post-hypnotic suggestions will lose their effect within a very short**

**time unless reinforced frequently.** Her volunteers would've been able to resist or forget that "The British are coming" within a day or so.

So, if you're the client we talked about that wants to quit smoking, the suggestion that *cigarettes taste terrible and make everything reek of smoke* will last for a while, but unless you have continuing visits with the hypnotist or they teach you how to reinforce that "suggestion" for yourself, it'll soon wear off and everything will be back to the way it was before.

I know you must be wondering, if your issue or post-hypnotic suggestion is from childhood, why hasn't it worn off?" Very simple. It's been continually *reinforced by you* with self-talk.

## It's All You

Good news is we can change any aspect of our personalities or behavior if we want to, because the fact of the matter is there's no such thing as being hypnotized by another person. All the other person does is make certain suggestions and you either accept them or reject them.

For example, if the hypnotist says, "Your eyelids are getting heavy," you have two choices. You can either accept the suggestion by saying, "Yes, my eyelids are getting heavy," in which case your body will respond to you and your eyelids will feel heavy, or you can say, "No, my eyelids are not getting heavy," in which case, nothing will happen.

All the hypnotist does is tell you *how* to do it. So, in fact, **you hypnotize yourself** by your consistent self-talk. "It's hard for me to lose weight. I just can't do it." Or "I'll never lose weight." Do those comments sound familiar to you? Remember, you'll always believe what your inner voice tells you, even if it puts you down… *especially* if it puts you down.

That explains how you've been constantly reinforcing your post-hypnotic suggestion ever since it's origin.

> **REMEMBER, YOU'LL ALWAYS BELIEVE WHAT YOUR INNER VOICE TELLS YOU.**

We'll be working on breaking the pattern in a few different upcoming chapters. However, first we need to start with identifying the things you keep doing or saying to yourself over and over again so we know what you're working with.

Here are some examples of the results of repeated actions and attitudes… patterns that are not productive. Recognize any?

- I'm the same 30 lbs. overweight that I was last year.

- I always spend more money than I make.

- I'm still in the same dead-end job I vowed to get out of last year.

- I have great ideas, but I never follow them through to completion.

- When I'm trying to make a sale, I can never bring myself to ask for the order to close it.

- People never take me seriously because I always turn everything into a joke, including myself.

Now it's your turn. What are yours?

Think about it. Write them down.

It might be painful, but by identifying and acknowledging it, you're breaking the pattern and taking the power back!

# CHAPTER 15

# OH WHERE, OH WHERE, DID MY SELF-ESTEEM GO?

*"You, yourself, as much as anybody in the entire Universe, deserve your love and affection."*

Buddha

In the movie, "I Feel Pretty", the main character is an insecure woman with devastatingly low self-esteem. After suffering a head injury, she wakes up with the belief that her appearance has magically changed and she is now the most beautiful, most capable woman on the planet. She approaches her new world with uber confidence. But in reality, the only thing that had truly changed was her mind…her attitude about herself.

When the lead actress Amy Schumer was being interviewed, she said that with her character's blow to the head, she all of a sudden had "little girl confidence." You know, how kids let their belly's hang out in a shirt too small and they walk proudly, feeling like the prettiest girl or best-looking boy on the planet. That's the innocent confidence we lose as we get older because of the things other people say, or the things that happen to us that slowly chisel away at that childlike confidence and lead to low self-esteem.

True belief in your ability to achieve your goals and live your best life, depends on your level of positive self-esteem…your confidence in you. In that movie, the characters self-esteem was off the charts, she *believed* she could do anything and therefore was unstoppable.

Before we move on let me make sure you understand what self-esteem really is. **Self-Esteem is what you think of yourself.** Your self-love! Your self-confidence and self-worth.

Deepak Chopra says "When you focus on the internal timeless and greater reality of our true being, then that self is fearless, beneath no one, and is immune to caring what other's think of us"…like a child's confidence, with their belly's hanging out. We achieve self-esteem through self-awareness. Your self-esteem will be through the roof after all the self-awareness you get from reading this book, right? That's the idea.

Low self-esteem is more of a problem now than it ever was due to being constantly scrutinized, shamed and sometimes bullied on social media platforms. I saw a study where 60% of people using social media reported that it's impacted their self-esteem in a negative way.

Some age groups have had a relationship with the internet and social media their whole lives. The young rapper "Chika" said she was literally raised by it. It taught her to seek validation based on engagement, and when your engagement declines, so does your mental health. She's learned over time and experiences, to be her authentic self and not seek validation. That girl is wise beyond her years.

Think about how many people, including children, have "been raised by it" and have their heads buried in their phone, tablets and computers mesmerized by social media for hours. That's a lot of humans' self-esteem taking a daily blow.

## Online Bullying

Pop star Selena Gomez cancelled her world tour a few years ago and went to therapy because she was depressed, anxious and her "Self-esteem was shot." She was having panic attacks on the tour because she felt she "Wasn't good enough, wasn't capable and wasn't giving the fans what they wanted." On top of that, online bullies were commenting on her weight and appearance while she was dealing with the effects of the autoimmune disease Lupus on her physical and mental health. Even on the re-make of the TV show "Saved by the Bell," they made fun of her and her kidney transplant needed due to Lupus. Really? People just plain suck sometimes. Keeping it real.

It was bad enough back in the day with regular societal ideals we all tried to live up to, and bullies on the playground… but now it's gone way beyond the playground, with worldwide cyber bullying and even TV shows, apparently. If someone is a victim of abuse, they get trapped in the post hypnotic suggestions of that victimization; helplessness, negative thinking, shame, and depression to name a few. It's such an epidemic, children are literally killing themselves over being cyber bullied.

Thing is, way before social media had such an influence on us, we already had post hypnotic suggestions forming self-esteem issues and an inadequate self-image from events in our childhood, we just weren't aware of it. I realize not everyone had a childhood filled with traumatizing events. I

> WE ACHIEVE SELF-ESTEEM THROUGH SELF AWARENESS.

certainly didn't, but there *are* certain events during our childhood that we aren't even consciously aware of that can unknowingly be holding us back. Those events, and the conditioning we received growing up has a lasting effect on our self-image and can be a roadblock all by itself, hindering our success and quality of life. It starts *much* earlier than you think.

## It Starts As Early As 42 Minutes Old

"No Small Matter" is an outstanding documentary on childhood learning and development. It's available on Amazon and I think this should be required viewing for every parent, grandparent, educator and anyone else who has an influence on children. It shows the immediate life altering effects a baby's surrounding in the early years makes on the rest of their lives.

It proves that babies start learning the minute they're born. A mind-blowing example of this in the documentary, is a scene of a doctor with a baby that's 42 minutes old. Yes…only 42 minutes. To prove the theory, the doctor sticks out his tongue at her…she immediately sticks out her tongue back at him. He opens his mouth wide…she opens her mouth wide. **The baby hasn't been in the world even an hour and is already learning how to imitate others behavior.**

Dr. Nadine Burke Harris, a pediatrician and the Surgeon General of California, talks about the scientific fact that our brains grow the most during the first 5 years of life, showing the importance of choosing the right people for your baby to be around, always of course, but especially their first 5 years.

It's during those first 5 years that our experiences literally shape our brains. If your healthy experiences are disrupted or even missed, for whatever reason, it weakens your foundation and your brain will have to deal with it the rest of your life. A baby's early experiences and the connections they have with the important adults in their lives during this time of incredible brain development creates the foundation for ALL that follows. Meaning the rest of their lives from 5 years old on!

According to Dr. Harris, if we don't get those first 5 right, inadequate self-images begin to form subconsciously and from that point on, we're basically fixing what's been broken.

That is why this book exists…to help you fix what's broken and rebuild your broken self-esteem.

## Daddy's Helper

As we start to grow up and try new experiences, we hear many "do's and don'ts," leading to feelings of either confidence or inadequacy… scientifically referred to as "conditioning." That conditioning is what can cause the limiting beliefs and post hypnotic suggestions to start stacking up against you.

Here's an example of conditioning; parents, pay close attention.

As a little boy, Johnny goes out to the garage where his father is working in his woodshop. Fascinated, he watches his father as he's making something. Soon, watching isn't enough. He wants to "help." At this point two different scenarios can happen…one will result in positive conditioning… the other will hurt his self-image and affect his development as he grows up into adulthood.

If his father gives him some safe but satisfying simple task to do, lets him do it, guides him to some small success, and then praises his efforts, the boy's self-image has received a big boost. If that pattern is repeated again and again, confidence is built through the habit of success and will help him build a self-image that is continually growing stronger.

But, if on the other hand, "Daddy's" time and patience is short, and Johnny's interest and desire to participate only irritates his dad, his dad's response could cause irreparable harm to the boys self-image. His repeated efforts to "help" daddy may result in being sent away from the garage as punishment for what his dad sees as disobedience…instead of eagerness to learn, and desire to just be with his dad and "help" him.

Either way, the child's been taught a lesson. Either it's been a positive experience boosting his self-esteem, or he's been taught or "conditioned" into a belief that he's not good at a certain kind of activity, or that he's not good just because he wanted to participate. Basically *"bad"* because he was *ambitious.*

This story brings us back to post-hypnotic suggestions. Imagine all the "suggestions" and roadblocks this kid will have as he gets older because of this one experience.

## Can You Believe?

As an adult, all of those limiting behaviors, post hypnotic suggestions and conditioning can subconsciously lead to an inadequate self-image holding you back from your best life.

Remember we did a little test back in Chapter Four when I asked you to verbally declare that all debts would be paid, and you'd have $50,000 in the bank? It was a brief example of the doubt and limiting beliefs that can be caused by your inadequate self-image.

In his original book, Joe used the real-life example of an advertising account of his, a real estate firm, to explain the power of an inadequate self-image. The real estate firm was expanding and wanted to attract some new, top salespeople. So, they placed an ad truthfully stating that people who were willing to work for them could earn over $100,000 a year.

The ad brought in no one. Not one applicant. So, they changed *one word* and placed the ad again. This time they ended up with more candidates than they knew what to do with. The word, or really the figure, they changed was "$100,000." They made it "$40,000" instead. They lowered the salary potential by $60,000 and the applicants came in droves! Isn't that crazy? The first ad failed because very few people could believe they were worth $100,000 a year so they didn't even bother answering the first ad.

## Again...It's About You

We live out our self-fulfilling prophecies based upon the *image* we have of ourselves. We tell ourselves I'm a good cook, but a lousy mechanic; or I'm great at English but suck at math. We can tell ourselves we're not worthy of a $100,000 job, and let it keep us stuck in our smallness. Or not! Good news is it's only **your** belief that you buy into, so you can change your belief and change your world.

Again, it's a shift in Attitude....Again, its how you talk to yourself... Again, you have control. Are you starting to see a pattern of who has the power to make changes?

## How You Doing?

So, where are you with your self-esteem? Is it broken? You are not alone my friend, but don't let those years of negative conditioning get in the way of doing something positive about your future. Don't be surrounded by your glass walls. **Those walls are just echoes of past post-hypnotic suggestions by others and yourself.** It's never too late to fix the brokenness.

To establish real self-esteem, concentrate on your *growth* towards a better you. Ignore the bullies, including the worst one of all that you'll learn about in the next chapter. Remember it's the bullies that have the lowest self-esteem of all.

> IT'S NEVER TOO LATE TO FIX THE BROKENNESS.

You can start now by making an intentional effort to become more aware of your behavior, your personal habits, your posture, and appearance. In whatever you do, try to do it just a little better each time. Always try for your personal best in everything.

Get back to that child like confidence.

Love yourself. Trust yourself. Respect yourself. Show up strong for yourself. Your self-esteem will grow as you continue to grow.

# THE DAILY MIND F**K

*"Be mindful of your self-talk.
It's a conversation with the universe."*

David James Lees

Who is the most influential person in your life? Who do you listen to more than anyone? Who do you always agree with even when they put you down? You!

## The Daily Mind F**K

We've talked about bullies and toxic people, but what most people don't understand is that we can become toxic to *ourselves* by self-bullying.

We talk to ourselves all day, every day. Not necessarily out loud, I'm talking about silent sentences. It's called self-talk and it's one of the universal roadblocks to achieving goals and living your best life. These silent sentences are influenced by your subconscious mind and reveal your true thoughts and beliefs. Most of the time it's negative self-talk, the brainwashing of post hypnotic suggestions from your past, holding you back from moving forward; doubts, limiting beliefs, fears and talking down to ourselves…self-verbal abuse. Yes, abuse. The kind of talk we'd stop someone else from saying if we saw it being said to another human…Bullying.

You can do all the steps I've said, but if you constantly tell yourself that you're not worthy, it's going to stop you in your tracks because **you start to believe the steady, daily drumbeat of that self-verbal abuse…the daily mind f\*\*k.** No one can thrive under that.

## Stop Self-Bullying!

Motivational author Bob Proctor says, "Don't be a victim of negative self-talk. Remember *you* are listening."

That mirrors what I've been saying all along, that you always believe what you tell yourself.

We are our own toughest critic, and on top of that we pile on more drama by listening to others and letting their words affect us. Other's words can absolutely hurt us, but it's how we *internalize* their words and add them to our own internal daily self-bullying that eventually brings us down.

Nicole Scherzinger, the beautiful and talented singer, and judge on the TV show, "The Masked Singer," is just one of many celebrities that battled self-bullying. She told herself that she was fat, wasn't pretty and that she wasn't worthy of more. I'm sorry, what?

Can you imagine a friend saying that to you? Of course not. You'd tell them to f\*\*k off right, and yet somehow, we all seem to think it's ok to speak to ourselves that way. Well it's not. Didn't your mom say, "If you can't say something nice about someone, don't say anything at all?" Mine sure did. If I said something "not nice," I got my mouth washed out with soap. Yes, it really was a thing back in the day, and in my opinion

> **PUTTING ANYONE DOWN, INCLUDING YOURSELF, IS EMOTIONAL BULLYING.**

still should be. But I digress…point is **putting anyone down, including yourself, is emotional bullying!**

We talked about self-esteem in the last chapter. Well, Emma Watson, the actress best known for her role as Hermione in the "Harry Potter" movie series, said she was completely overwhelmed by her self-esteem issues when she was younger. At 21 she didn't like photos being taken of herself. She was full of insecurities and self-critiquing and one day realized it was because she had trouble dealing with the glamorous images of herself on magazine covers. Comparing the girl on the cover who had people doing makeup, hair, lighting and wardrobe…to her normal self without all of that fuss, made her feel inadequate. And she thought if she can't even live up to herself, how is anyone else meant to live up to those magazine images? Amen.

It's not a surprise. We're all constantly bombarded with unrealistic images from social media, or the airbrushed beauties in print magazines to try and live up to. I grew up with a very real, very beautiful former Miss America as a stepmom, so trust! I did a lot of self bullying because I didn't look like her…an American icon for goodness sakes. Who can live up to that? She never made me feel anything less than beautiful. I did that self-verbal abuse all by myself for years. My own mind f\*\*k until I built up my self-esteem.

## The Not So Funny Put Down

So, to protect ourselves we use defense mechanisms to deal. We pick on areas where we feel insecure such as looks, weight, age or intelligence and make fun of ourselves before anyone else does. We think that if we laugh about these things first, then others will laugh *with* us and not *at* us. Think about the stereotype of the overweight kid who becomes a comedian because they used humor to make fun of themselves so others wouldn't.

Do you ever find yourself making fun of yourself in front of friends about something you're self-conscious about? Say, you make a joke that you hope a chair can hold your weight, because deep down you're uncomfortable about your weight. We all do that sometimes about whatever our hang-up is. It's easy to fall back into that post hypnotic pattern. It's a defense mechanism against criticism and fear of rejection but it's really self-bullying disguised as comic relief.

The problem with this is that our subconscious mind has no sense of humor. It treats everything we tell it as real, remember? So those things we laughingly say about ourselves, the subconscious takes seriously which reinforces the insecurities we're trying to hide in the first place.

If you've fallen into this trap of throwing epic shade at yourself, you'll never change as long as you keep reinforcing it with self-bullying.

## Don't Use The Weed Killer

Self-doubt also falls into this area of self-talk. The doubt we hold in our minds can hold us back in our lives.

Think about the doubting self-talk as you go for say, your goal of financial freedom. You have a daily declaration for financial freedom…you *say the words* in your morning and evening success routine…but yet in the back of your mind you're still doubting the process as you continue to stress and work out how you're *really* going to pay your debts.

You can be doing all the steps to change your life, but if you continue to doubt and think about debt, you're wishing and working towards something on one hand...but cancelling it out with your thoughts on the other hand. As author Peggy McColl puts it, **you're planting a healthy seed and then putting weed killer on it.**

You can mind f**k yourself right out of the daily declarations, super suggestions and all natural laws in existence with that self-doubt and negative self-talk.

## Do I Need To Get The Soap?
Having said that, I know no sane person would consciously choose to do a daily self-sabotage. It comes from not being aware of your self-bullying and the effect it has on you.

So, now that you know, start paying attention to what comes out of your mouth as you speak to yourself. Try it for a day. **Be self-aware of your *dis*-empower statements** that continually reinforce false and limiting beliefs and attitudes about yourself; the ones where you use the "I can't' s," and the "I am's." As in statements like "*I am* horrible at math" or "*I am* fat and out of shape." or "*I can't* because I'm not smart enough." You'll be genuinely surprised to see how often you say something about yourself that **you would call someone else a bully for saying to you or anyone else.**

To build your self-esteem, it's important to talk about yourself in a healthy way. You're the creator of your thoughts and beliefs, and you have the power at any moment to choose the ones that are life-enhancing rather than self-limiting. Quit the self-bullying. You're better than that. Do I need to get the soap?

## Teach Others How To Treat You

Another way self-bullying has an effect on your life is how you let others treat you. Dr. Phil McGraw says we teach others how to treat us. He's right. Other people react to you the way you tell them to. Not verbally of course, but by your actions and appearance. If others see you not respecting yourself, you won't get a whole lot of respect from them. That isn't only how you speak to yourself, or how you let others speak to you, it's how you present yourself as well.

What you do, how you act, your posture, your punctuality, the way you dress, or the way you introduce yourself, tells other people how to treat you. They will, in almost every case, go along with you. If you expect respect and consideration, you'll get it. If you don't, you won't. It's that simple. So show up early, dressed sharp, standing confident, and have a firm handshake while looking them in the eye. Trust. You'll get respect if you do those things, and they'll pay attention to you from that point on.

## Positive Self-Talk

The important thing to realize is that you're in control. So, take charge of your self-talk, and have it start working for you, instead of against you.

In the sports world, research supports the fact that an athlete who consistently uses self-talk will improve their sports performance…that replacing negative self-talk with positive self-enhancing talk is the key to either winning or not.

It's true in the military too. In Oprah's magazine, a former Navy SEAL Command Master Chief said that positive self talk is quite possibly the most important skill the SEALS learn during their 15-month training. The most successful SEALS know how to turn their negative thoughts around. For them, it's literally a matter of survival. They come up with their own mantra to remind themselves that they've got the grit and talent to persevere through tough times. It's just as true with you…it's a matter of survival.

And it's true with celebrities. Jennifer Lopez once did an interview with TV talk show host Meredith Viera and talked about her previous low self-esteem issues. Yes, *that* J-Lo. Hard to imagine right? But it just goes to show you that everyone faces issues with low self-esteem at some point in their lives brought about by self-doubt, which is brought on by self-bullying. She explained that in a world of judgements and critics, including ourselves, it's common to feel low and have doubts about yourself.

So how did she cope? She switched it up to constant positive self-talk and daily affirmations. She used to tell herself, "I'm going to make another record. I'm a great actress, I'm a great singer, a great dancer. I'm great at this stuff, and I'm going to keep going!" She did her daily declarations and it worked. It'll work for you too.

## Empower Yourself

The reason for the daily mind f**k is listening to others and not feeling we measure up, and listening to ourselves about why we feel we don't measure up.

If you want to change your mind, you have to change what you tell yourself. You need to involve your *conscious* mind through the use of the daily declarations and through constant attention to your self-talk. I've already suggested you pay attention to your *dis*-empowerment comments. I now want you to learn to replace those negative "I can'ts" and "I am's" with positive self-supporting statements.

For example…instead of saying, "I am too fat and out of shape" say, "I am working on my weight with exercise as part of my morning success routine."

Instead of saying, "I can't afford it" say, "I am accumulating all the money I need for this or anything else that I want."

It may sound cheesy to your conscious mind, but it won't to your subconscious and that's the one that matters, because it's real to your subconscious and this method works.

Finally, I saw this technique for stopping negative self-verbal abuse on the internet and it was too good to not share with you.

## S.O.S

### ( 1 )  Stop

Mentally tell yourself "Stop!" to give you the opportunity to address the thought and interrupt the cycle.

### ( 2 )  Observe

Observe what you're saying to yourself and how it's making you feel.

### ( 3 )  Shift

Shift your cognitive emotional or behavioral response by using positive coping skills and techniques.

Remember this quote as you go through the daily work of changing how you talk to yourself.  It's a Mind HUG!

> *"What I want you to remember is to talk to yourself like you would to someone you love!"*
>
> Brene' Brown

# YOU'VE GOT SOME UNPACKING TO DO

*"It's easier traveling the road of life
when I don't have so much to carry on my back."*

Silas Weir Mitchell

*Empathy: "Let me hold the door for you.*
*I may have never walked in your shoes, but I can see your soles are worn,*
*your strength is torn under the weight of a story I have never lived before.*
*Let me hold the door for you.*
*After all you've walked through, it's the least I can do."*

Morgan Harper Nichols

I felt the need to open this chapter about "baggage" with this beautiful piece about empathy because we cover some deep s**t. Some that I've "lived" before, and for those I share my stories to let you know you're not alone. On the things I haven't, I have heartbreaking empathy. Either way, I want to "hold the door" for you and guide you through to the other side of the threshold, where your strength is renewed. After all you've walked through…it's the least I can do.

Baggage. We all have it. Some are loaded down more than others, but whether we're consciously aware of it or not, rich or poor, if it's Louis Vuitton bags or a bag from the Ross sale rack. …we're all carrying some.

What kind of baggage am I talking about? That accumulation of undealt with emotions and trauma, creating emotional baggage that pushes you into a smaller life. You know the bags; fear, bad habits, toxic relationships, trauma drama, or attitudes like the daily mind f**k we just discussed.

When discussing this with a friend who is a fierce survivor of generational trauma, she said she has "packed up her feelings in a suitcase since she was a child and has carried them around her whole life, stuffing more in along the journey." Well, there reaches a point where that baggage begins busting open at the seams, and you have to start unpacking. Now is that time.

We're all shaped by our life experiences. For some, it starts with childhood hurts and trauma that we may or may not remember. For others, it's built up from words or experiences that happen later in life. Those experiences are what shape our attitudes and choices that become baggage, like hanging on to a fear that's holding you back, or holding on to a secret because you're ashamed.

> **DO YOU WANT TO KEEP LETTING YOUR BAGGAGE KEEP YOU FROM YOUR BEST LIFE?**

Whatever the origin, we've become so used to living with it that we become blind to it and don't recognize the damage being done. Or we *do* recognize it but become comfortably numb because it's easier to go numb than it is to confront the feeling and have to do something about it. And that's where the problem lies, you hold on to it and let it weigh you down every day, impacting the way you show up for work, for love and for life.

## A Time For Healing

So, the question is…do you want to keep letting your baggage keep you from your best life?

No?

Good. Enough is enough, right? Liberate the inner child, the one with the bags. The baggage is all crap from the past. We can't change the past of course, but we can absolutely change the future by choosing to let go of it. If the Covid19 pandemic has taught us anything, it's reminded us of how precious our time is. There's enough stuff in our life that we can't control…why not be boss over the things you can?

You're learning the tools to be able to handle this now, so let's talk about the things weighing you down, face them, deal with them and move on so you have the bandwidth to start recognizing and nourishing those things in life that uplift you.

It won't be easy. We're going to have some serious real talk. It's not easy to unpack years of your life, but now is the time to love yourself and the loved ones in your life enough to start. So, we'll start unpacking here, and in the following three chapters by talking about the things that don't get talked about. Maybe it's a bad habit you've been embarrassed about, maybe you need that kick in the butt to get rid of toxic waste in your life, or maybe it's generational trauma that you weren't consciously aware of that has been holding you back possibly your whole life.

This is your safe place. Change begins with awareness, so I'm here to make you aware that it's time for that change.

## Don't Sweat The Small Stuff

Some of that baggage often starts over something small and can grow to sizes disproportionate to the situation. I call that small minded baggage.

Can we just talk about the Hatfield's and McCoy's for a minute? For those that don't know, the Hatfield's and McCoy's are the subjects of a well-known generational family feud that has become a part of Americana. Google it. There are several reports about how it started but the most widely accepted is, are you ready for this…a McCoy hog, *one* hog, was stolen by a Hatfield. Yep, that one small thing led to a downright war between them for over 20 years. WTF? That's a supersized reality check of how stupid little things can escalate into bigger stupid things.

I know your things may feel big to you, as that hog being stolen apparently felt to McCoy, but these first few I'll talk about are really a matter of attitude that some of you have let escalate into baggage. ..small minded baggage.

So, let's start off easy with that small mind baggage. **These first few are the things Eeyore's are made of.** I'm not going to spend a lot of time on these because when you get down to it, one shift in attitude and you can let it go… and we have way bigger bags to get to. Just keeping it real.

## Small Minded Attitude Baggage

> **Envy…**rooted in insecurity and low self-esteem. You don't need to be envious of anyone, you can get your own, as you're learning.
>
> **Jealousy…**also rooted in insecurity and low self-esteem, and is one of the most destructive. It destroys the love that it's supposedly trying to protect. The solution is not in restricting someone else's behavior, it's raising your own concept of yourself. If you're lucky enough to find love, don't drag it down, nurture it and be thankful.

**Bitterness and Resentment...** Being bitter and holding resentment towards someone doesn't do anything to the person you're resenting, it only harms you, your health and your quality of life. Simply release all feelings of anger, bitterness and revenge no matter how justified you think they are. Forgiveness is life changing and you have the power to do it. It's never too late.

**Prejudice...** rooted in insecurity, low self-esteem and is the most egregious of the small mind baggage. It's something I can't speak to because I will NEVER understand hating someone because of the color of their skin, where they came from, who they choose to love, how they choose to identify themselves or who they worship. If this is you, I can only pray for you and suggest that you really look at yourself. Is it how you *really* feel or is it what others have taught you that you've gone along with? It's never too late to change.

Let go of your past and your small minded attitudes and move on with your life. It's a conscious choice. It's a simple mind shift. When you give yourself an attitude adjustment you'll feel better about yourself, and you'll feel lighter.

Next let's move on to two medium sized bags...Fear and Guilt.

# Fear

Has fear pushed you into a smaller life? Fear can stop us in our tracks and strip us of our power. Don't give it that power. You may have let it stop you before, but now you're learning the tools needed to deal with the glass walls and roadblocks from yesterday that caused fear. Your self-esteem is growing, giving you the confidence to say "Bye Felicia" to the attitudes, limiting beliefs and post-hypnotic suggestions that cause fear. You've discovered that you have the power and strength inside of you to take that power back.

Having said that, fear of the unknown is one of the biggies and the Covid19 pandemic has triggered it in even the strongest people. Here's the problem...putting our energy into feeding that fear just makes it worse.

Our resident life coach, Donna Quarles of itstimetosoar.com, created this dead-on acronym for FEAR that she uses to make her clients realize that they have the power when it comes to dealing with their fears.

## FEAR = Fighting Energy Against Reality! — Energy = FAR!

Truth, right? When we use up our energy to **fight** the **reality** of whatever is causing our fear, it just makes it worse. We need to take the E out of fear...the Energy...to go to **FAR!** In the case of Covid19 for instance, it's a reality and fighting it isn't going to help. What does help is putting that energy into being informed and taking the right precautions to be safe until we as a world get a handle on this thing. I did that by controlling what I can, and by getting the vaccine.

That acronym or theory works on most situational fears, as does a process Life Coach Iyanla from the OWN network uses with her clients dealing with fears;

She says to **Name the Fears.** Ask yourself, *what's the worst that could happen?* and then ask yourself, *if that happens, then what? And then what?*

The goal is to work the fear down. If what you fear did come to pass, would it really be as terrible as you imagined? If so, how would you address it? What would you do to cope?

Often by simply identifying the fear and figuring out a concrete way to deal with it should it come true, you remove its power to control your decision making. Therefore, making the decision yours and giving the energy and power back to you. The decision to face it and work through it is what gives you the strength to slam the doors of fear. So, go slam some doors, will you?

> ...IT'S NEVER LOCKED AWAY FROM *YOU.*

## Guilt

Guilt is a tough one. If you're a parent and feel guilty about having to work and leave your child, I get it. Or if you have guilt and shame about bad choices you've made, or the "ugly" habits that affected others lives along with yours, I understand. 100%. That's completely normal and a healthy reaction.

What isn't healthy is to hold onto it and let it hold you back or dictate your happiness. Holding on to the past and wallowing in guilt doesn't help anyone, especially you. Like I said before…don't keep diggin' up that grave. Accept responsibility for whatever you feel guilty about, and make the adjustments you can.

Parents…make the most of the time you do have with your child. Don't all sit in front of mind numbing tv or your phones longing after others Insta lives. Get a life. Read with your kids, go outside and play or take a walk together and just…wait for it…talk.

If you had an ugly habit that caused drama or trauma for others, or hurt someone with words…or whatever is causing your guilt, do what you can to repair the damage that was done, learn the lessons from your mistakes, ask forgiveness, work hard to not do it again and move forward. It's never too late.

I could write a book on this alone…but you get the idea. I need to move on to two of the bigger bags.

## The Heavier Bag's...

I'm just going to rip the band aid off, because there are times when not facing or talking about your problem leads to a bigger problem that turns into some of the heaviest baggage. People hold onto dark traumatic experiences…secrets they've locked away. But though it's locked away from others, **it's never locked away from you**. You're processing it and being affected by it every day. It can cause you to block out a certain part of you and your heart, causing depression and anxiety to where you become a shell of your authentic self.

## Shame

Shame, one of the biggest, usually isn't talked about which is why it becomes one of the heaviest bags of all. Shame comes from experiences that are too often kept secret and legit are too big to unpack by only reading a chapter in a book. I realize that but I want to acknowledge it and discuss it here where it's safe so the healing process can start.

Shame can come from so many life experiences that boil down to three main reasons…a secret you hold on to because *something was done to you*…or from *something you've done to others* that may or may not be so secret…or *something you do to yourself* that probably affects others. Whatever the scenario, it will eat at you from the inside until it is faced and worked through.

If it's something you're doing to yourself that affects your life and possibly others, find the help you need to stop. Seriously. Don't let it continue to escalate into the many longer, windier, scarier paths it could take you. It's never too late.

If it's something you did to someone else and have gone through the hard work to make sure it doesn't happen to anyone again…ask forgiveness of yourself and those you hurt. If not forgiven right away, stay patient and more importantly, consistent in your new behavior and it may eventually start to be noticed and walls will start falling down piece by piece. If forgiveness is never granted, the hurt may be too big and the other people involved have some work to do on their end, but at least you know you've done all the right things to amend it and move forward with your best life.

# #MeToo

If it's from something that was done to you, my goal is to make you understand that there's absolutely nothing to be ashamed about. You're not alone, #metoo, #itspersonal, and now is the time to love yourself enough to face it, deal with it, and talk to someone to help you move through it. Take the power back. Let me tell you a short story I read in *Vouge* magazine about someone who did just that;

Olympic gymnast Simone Biles was sexually abused by her Olympic Team physician, as were over 90 young women by the same monster. She kept the assault to herself, holding on to the shame and guilt deep inside. Over a year later, she still hadn't processed what had happened to her and during that time she realized she had a lot of issues she didn't have prior to the abuse. At the time, her behavior and mood seemed inexplicable to her because she usually has such drive and discipline. She realized later that it was because the shame was buried so far down inside it was consuming her.

According to her, it was a really dark time. She had anxiety and was so depressed she went through a period of sleeping all day because it was the closest thing to death without harming herself. For her it was an escape from all of her thoughts, from the world and from what she was dealing with.

Until the story came out in the press, she hadn't considered her abuse to be "*actual* abuse" because she "didn't think it was bad as what others had gone through." She and her silent sentences had talked herself into feeling "like it didn't really happen because it wasn't so bad."

She realized in retrospect she didn't want to admit it to herself because she felt like she was expected to be perfect. She was afraid she would disappoint not only her family, but in her case, the world, because of her celebrity status as a strong, fierce world class athlete. She knew people would say 'How could she have let that happen to her?' She actually felt like she was letting *other* people down.

That breaks my heart because as crazy as that sounds, that's more often the case than not. So many victims of abuse, no matter what, who, when and how…blame themselves, stay silent and find unhealthy mechanisms to cope which causes some of the habits we'll talk about in Chapter Twenty. And some of those habits become another reason for shame and guilt.

But to truly be your best you and live your best life, you have to look at it. Face it head on with therapy or counseling of some kind. It's empowering. Emotional pain is something we can let control us if we don't deal with it, **but the minute you put a voice to your story, the shame has no power and you're back in control!**

Simone Biles finally came forward and posted about her abuse on Twitter. She said it was so liberating to share it and relieve herself of "a weight she carried so heavily on my chest." And she knew that by sharing her story, she would help others feel safe in coming forward to.

When you use your voice, that's how you make lasting change. So, if you're holding on to shame, please get help. Use your voice to tell your story to a therapist, a counselor or whomever you trust to help you through it. **There is no shame in that. Only Strength!** It's never too late.

## Depression

Depression and shame often go together, like Simone faced. All of the things I've discussed in this chapter, and some I will discuss in the next three chapters, can contribute to depression so I want to call it out here as we move forward.

I have not "walked in these shoes" so to speak, so I won't even try to give advice on the subject itself. I bring it up as a topic of discussion to raise awareness and let you know that if you're facing this, you're not alone. No matter who someone is or what kind of life someone has, no one is shielded from this. There is no reason to feel shame.

Depression is an illness that affects more than 264 million people worldwide according to the World Health Organization. According to

CNN, a 2020 Census Bureau survey found that one in three Americans reported symptoms of depression or anxiety. More than three times the rate from a similar survey in 2019.

Michelle Obama stated publicly in 2020 that she was experiencing a low-grade depression because of the pandemic and subsequent quarantine, racial injustice, and well…let's just say the political climate at that time. She was brave enough to say aloud what many people all over the world are experiencing right now, some for the first time.

With this pandemic, we've learned that significant disruptions to our everyday life can cause depression in people that may never have experienced it before. The seismic changes we're all adjusting to right now due to the daily devastation around the world has us in a roller coaster emotional state of highs and lows. Many are now homesick for the life they may have felt trapped in at the beginning of 2020, prepandemic.

On top of that, because of social distancing needed to fight this horrific pandemic, people have gone through long stretches of time without seeing their friends or family, which only exaggerates the already widespread problem of sadness, loneliness and anxiety that add to depression. I know my extrovert friends need interactions with other humans to refill their tank and not getting that can lead to depression.

For some like Michelle, depression is a new and hopefully temporary fact of life and will subside as these world struggles ease up, but for others it's been a long-time battle. As you've seen throughout this book, I use a lot of celebrity reference to humanize some of the points I'm trying to make, and unfortunately, I have countless to choose from regarding this subject. You just read about Simone's battle with it, for example.

Singer and American Idol Judge Katy Perry battled depression. She said she got caught up in the desperate loop of stardom and it took her out. She survived through medication and therapy.

Another is model and actress Cara Delevingne who went through a "Massive wave of depression, anxiety and self-hatred." In an interview she said she tried therapy and medication, but they didn't help which only made it worse. So, she turned to the ugly habits of drugs. She said, "I was packing my bags and suddenly I just wanted to end it." She had to decided "Whether I love myself as much as I love the idea of death." She chose to live.

Singer Demi Lovato and reality TV star Tamar Braxton made a different choice, but survived the attempts and got the help they needed. And then there are of course many that didn't…Robin Williams, Anthony Bourdain, …I actually just got overwhelmed trying to list a few more. I went to Google a few more names and the list of well-known people that committed suicide is so long it's actually an alphabetized list. If that doesn't show us what an overwhelming problem it is and that no one is shielded by it, I don't know what will.

I don't bring this up to depress you even more than you may already be. But, it's just us here so I wanted to take the opportunity to say out loud, so to speak, what may be troubling you in your heart and mind silently.

So, what can you do to battle it? I'm not qualified to offer advice on such a critical worldwide and yet deeply personal problem for so many, but what **I will tell you is what I would tell a friend that is dealing with this;**

For the depression caused by world issues, stop binge watching 24/7 news and news videos. That just makes it worse. It compounds day after day making it worse and leading to the feeling of helplessness, and even hopelessness which leads to depression. Take a walk outside in the fresh air instead, listen to music that uplifts you, a guided meditation, or a personal growth audio book.

Medications are of course a huge help but don't rely on them for the long term or that in itself can become baggage. The comedian Jim Carrey fought depression much of his life and at one time was on Prozac to help manage it, but said he had to get off it at a certain point. In his words, "You need to get out of bed every day and say that life is good." He said it was tough but got through it with a healthy diet and natural supplements for his improved mental health.

Michelle says for her, keeping a schedule is key. Maintaining a routine including exercise, getting fresh air and eating dinner at a routine time has helped her deal. BTW, that advice is also given by professional doctors that help others through this every day because being able to control certain things in your life, like dinner time, helps deal with those that you can't control like a worldwide unseen virus.

Most important, it's ok to acknowledge your depression. Not only ok, but it's absolutely necessary for your health and wellbeing. Allow yourself to be in your feels but talk to someone about them too so they don't take over and take you to darker places.

And most important to me, know that you my friend are worthy of the love and care you need to get through this. Love yourself enough to reach out to the many professionals that are available to talk to.

**After all you've walked through, let me open the door for you. There is a National Helpline offering free confidential service. Call them…please. 1.800.662.HELP (4357)**

**Demi Lovato shared an app that she used for help: Talkspace.com**

It's your choice. You have the control!

# BYE FELICIA!

*"People inspire you, or they drain you.
Pick them wisely."*

Hans F. Hanson

Alice Walker, the author of the novel *The Color Purple,* once said "No person is your friend who demands your silence or denies your right to grow." Amen!

I learned this the hard way with the first man in my love life. He was toxic with a capital "T." In our private world he was verbally abusive, constantly trying to belittle me and damage my self-esteem, and he succeeded. He was a wealthy, well-dressed, mild mannered *bully*. My young naïve eyes didn't see it for way too long, but I sure felt it. His constant toxicity wore me down emotionally until I lost myself and many of my friends. Worse, even when I eventually *did* see it, I still couldn't bring myself to leave. I was so beaten down emotionally I didn't have the strength.

I kept praying I'd "wake up" and have the strength to go. And then it happened. One glorious day my prayers were answered and the fog of doubt and insecurity in my head lifted. It became crystal clear what a loser he was, and I left his ass in a heartbeat. 2 years of my life wasted but I got out and got me back.

That was a lifetime ago, but it's a part of my story and it helped shape me into the strong woman I am today. One who learned the importance of choosing the right people to share this precious life with. It's why I'm so passionate about recognizing and getting rid of the toxic waste in *your* life. It's personal.

## Can You Move Around The Cabin Freely?

I say recognize, because the thing about toxic relationships is that when we're in them, we usually don't realize how damaging they are, like I didn't back in the day-day-day. This chapter is to help provide some clarity about who is toxic to you, and to help lift the fog of doubt and insecurity for those of you stuck in an unhealthy relationship and need a supportive nudge to get out. You deserve it.

## No one has the right to make you feel small or less than.

Spirit, the therapist seen often on "OWN" network says it this way; If you live in a world where you can't "move around the cabin freely," you're not really living your best life.

To be clear, not all toxic relationships are as blatantly damaging as straight up abuse. It can be deceptively subtle; a slow & steady beat down of your self-esteem, or someone who tries to prevent you from bettering yourself. Someone who keeps knocking you back down every time you start moving up, like the "whack-a-mole" game at an arcade. They try to keep you down so they feel better about themselves.

It may be a work relationship where you have to deal with an "Eeyore"… like a boss or a peer that leaves you drained and dreading going to work every day…or worse. I read an article about a woman who consistently went in to the bathroom to cry because of verbal abuse from a toxic boss. Oh hell no…no job is worth that! Boy, bye! Bye F'in' Felicia!

Or it's a family member or friend who has provided a lifetime of wearing your spirit down and killing your dreams one by one.

Does any of this sound familiar? I hope not but I know from experience it does to more of you than not. Whatever dark corner of our world they're lurking in, there's no doubt about it, there are people in our lives who are harmful to our emotional health and therefore, our physical health. Now is the time to recognize them and do something about it.

## Name Your Poison

Here's the good news…you have the power to do something about it and **you don't need anyone's permission.**

Remember the comment Whitney Houston made about her husband Bobby "dimming her light?" Well, I have 5 questions to help you identify those that are dimming *your* light, so we can weed them out of your life and make room for those that help you shine brighter.

Ask yourself these questions about the people in your life that you spend time with and have an impact on you; friends, work and personal relationships, teachers, family members, and I hate to say it but even some church leaders. Some will be obvious, while others may take a little more thought before you recognize the damage they're doing.

### Who am I around?
Who do I spend time with? Do I get to "move around the cabin freely" with them? Do they treat me with respect and support me **or** do they belittle and drain me?

**( 2 )** **Are they helping me be better or holding me back?**
Do they support my dreams or talk me out of them? Are they supporting me towards becoming the happier, healthier, more successful person I want to become **or** are they dragging me down, encouraging my bad unhealthy habits and holding me back from becoming a better me?

**( 3 )** **Do they want what's best for me?**
Or do they only take from me?

**( 4 )** **Are they affecting someone else I care about?**
A child for example.

**( 5 )** **Is that Ok with me?**
Do I want them to continue to have a negative impact on my life and anyone else in my life affected by this person?

The answers to those questions will make it obvious who should get the boot. A friend of mine calls it her "dead to me" list. One more thing that might help. Remember the quote I mentioned in an earlier chapter; "I'm making some changes in my life. If you don't hear from me…you're one of them!" Whoever comes to mind as you read that quote, needs to go.

Bye Felicia!

# And For Those You Can't Say "Bye Felicia" To...

Removing the toxic waste from your life is the best way to unpack and get on with your best life. Having said that, I realize that sometimes there are toxic people in your life that you just can't get away from like family members or your Eeyore boss of a job you just can't leave *yet*. If you can't say "Bye Felicia", you need to limit your time with them and make some adjustments to protect yourself. Here are a few ways to help you deal with those that try to make you feel less than, so **you keep the power**.

## KEEP THE POWER

- "Buttons" are a weakness. Toxic people push buttons deliberately to piss you off. They get a sick pleasure out of it because of their character weakness as a human. But here's the thing…someone can't push a button that they can't see. Stop yourself and breathe before reacting. Pause. Don't show emotion, and walk away. You can go in the bathroom and scream or cry after, but do not show emotion at the time. If you ignore them and walk away, **you keep the power**.

- Don't take people's words and actions to heart. Their words have nothing to do with you. If someone comes at you with disrespect or abuse…it shows how low their self-esteem is and they are envious of you or threatened by you, so they try to hold you down. You don't have to show up for the fight. You have the right to remove yourself from the conversation and **keep the power**.

- Don't ever let the toxic jerk stand over you or corner you. Ever! Stand at eye level if possible and always look them straight in the eye to show you won't back down and they cannot dominate you. **Keep the power.**

- If someone is always trying to manipulate you, take from you and make you feel inferior, find your voice and tell them NO. Stand strong and **take your power back**.

- If there's physical or verbal abuse, stand up for yourself and tell them you don't allow people to treat you this way, and leave. Something I wish I had said back in the day-day-day. I don't care who it is, that toxic waste needs a "Bye Felicia." **Take your power back!**

## Find Those Who Help You Shine Brighter

Mark Twain said to "'Keep away from people who try to belittle your ambitions…the really great people make you feel that you too can become great."

As you get rid of the toxic people in your life, replace them with positive people who live the kind of life you want and are examples of the person you want to become. People who make you feel that you too can be great.

Think about it, how do you feel when you're around people who are positive, enthusiastic and supportive? It's contagious right? They make you feel encouraged, inspired and fearless, like you can do anything.

Wouldn't you rather hang out with people like that? Well, news flash… you can. You have that right. The right to decide who's in your tribe.

So, work on creating a healthy environment for yourself. Build a support system that'll help you get where it is you want to go.

Rediscover friends and family that fell by the wayside because they wanted the best for you and couldn't support the toxic drama you were in. Trust! They'll love supporting the new and stronger you. Find new friends who want what you want, or at the very least understand it and support you. Find a mentor to help lift you up the ladder of success.

Elizabeth David said, "There are people who take the heart out of you, and there are people who put it back." Let me help you find the ones who put it back.

Just as I asked those 5 questions to identify the toxic people in your life, I have 5 questions to ask yourself as you select new friends and create your new tribe.

**1** **Who brings out the best in you?**
Who stimulates and encourages your gifts, creativity and talent?

**2** **Who energizes you?**

**3** **Who is a giver—not a taker?**

**4** **Who supports you even when they don't agree with you?**

**5** **Who do you maintain your sense of self with?**
Who lets you "do you?"

## Like Attracts Like

There are so many counseling groups and networking groups to be a part of. Reach out to them or join our private Facebook community @ nopermissionsociety. As you increase your associations with nourishing people, you'll feel better about yourself and about your ability to move forward with your dreams and best life. It creates a snowball effect. That new confidence will attract more positive people in your life. It's the Law of Attraction. Like attracts like.

I understand this can all be overwhelming. I know it may not feel like it, but it's never too late. It may feel like you'll never be able to break those toxic chains. I promise you can. If you feel alone, like there's no one in your life that can support you or understands what you're going through... talk to your teacher, find a therapist or support group, or reach out to our life coaches for guidance. Whatever you need to do to make it happen...do it.

Whether its saying goodbye to the toxic waste or limiting your time with the toxic waste...now is your time to get *you* back. No one has the right to take your best life away from you. Focus on finding the ones who want you to have that best life and will stand by you supporting you as you go get it.

And when you *do* leave, because I *know* you can do it, be sure to talk to someone so you don't repeat the patterns and end up in another toxic situation. **I want you to unpack this baggage for good and burn the suitcase.**

It worked for me. After that toxic first relationship I mentioned at the beginning, I surrounded myself with the right people who encouraged me as I regained my confidence and strength. I eventually found my person who helped me shine brighter in love and life. It all started with taking the critical step of removing the toxic waste from my life that one glorious day. Now it's your turn.

And remember...always take care of yourself *and* the ones you are either responsible for, or can't take care of themselves...like children, our older generations or pets.

If you need to, reach out to the National Domestic Abuse Hotline at 1.800.799.7233 and www.thehotline.org

Whether it's them or one of the many other organizations out there to help, please reach out to someone who can help you start to unpack! Some anonymous internet wisdom I found says; "When you start seeing your worth, you'll find it harder to stay around people who don't." Amen!

Time to say Bye Felica and Hello World.

("Bye Felicia" is a reference to a line in the movie "Friday")

# THE TRICKLE-DOWN EFFECT

*"Pain travels through families
until someone is ready to feel it."*

Stephi Wagner

Sometimes the most important days of our lives, the ones that will impact our lives most dramatically, happen when we're not even there to see it… because we weren't even born yet. Let me explain.

When I was barely a teen, I went to help my grandmother cleanup after dinner one night. As I entered the kitchen, I saw her eating all the scraps of food left on each of our plates, in a secretive and desperate way as if the food would be taken away at any moment.

She didn't know I was there, and I instinctively knew she wouldn't want anyone seeing her, so I quietly retreated into the living room where I pulled my dad aside and asked him why she was doing that.

He explained that she was a "depression era baby." She grew up during the great depression when food was rationed and therefore scarce, and her parents fear of food insecurity "trickled down" to have a lifelong impact on her. Trust me when I say she would never have to worry about where her next meal came from at that point in her life, but clearly, she had a subconscious fear of not having enough to eat…still.

That was my first encounter with generational trauma and the trickle-down effect it has.

## The Trickle-Down Effect
So, what is Generational Trauma?

**A simplified explanation of Generational Trauma is an event that occurred years prior to the current generation, but still impacts the family today.** Meaning it's not only the individual that experiences trauma, but it's handed down to the children through behaviors, patterns and symptoms of the trauma, which causes it to then continue to trickle down through the family line the same way.

There's even scientific evidence to suggest we actually carry the impact of our ancestor's traumas in our DNA, going back at least three generations. The memories and trauma are *inherited*. The scientific term for this is Epigenetic Inheritance.

I have close friends that are self-proclaimed poster children for generational trauma, and chances are that someone in your life, maybe even your family, is affected by it.

WE ARE LIVING IN THE MIDST OF CULTURAL TRAUMAS RIGHT NOW.

I'm writing about it to bring awareness to this heavy baggage that so many carry without even knowing it, so action can be taken to make changes and break the cycle, because as with making most changes, awareness is the first step.

GT generally falls into two categories; Cultural and Individual.

## Cultural Trauma

Cultural traumas are those turning points in our history and culture that affect all of us and the generations that follow because of the mass scope of it.

The list of cultural traumas is unfortunately overwhelming, but Slavery, The Holocaust, Black Wall Street, the Great Depression and the attacks of 9/11 are just a few examples from the past. Think about the trickle-down effect of just those five on the generations since, and you get the idea of what I'm talking about.

Actually, we're all living in the midst of cultural trauma right now with two separate issues…one new and one painfully old; the Covid19 Pandemic, and the #blacklivesmatter, #sayhername, and #stopasianhate movements.

The Covid19 Pandemic has changed our world. It will never be the same after this. The pandemic has already changed the way we were living to a new norm that is here to stay. Just think of the trickle-down effect impacting our school aged children who's education alone is affected for the rest of their life.

Our world has had the cultural trauma of racism for generations back to …well forever, but the escalating, egregious brutality and killings of black lives and seeing them in live video feeds will absolutely cause a new layer of generational trauma on a massive scope. How can you not be traumatized by this no matter what race you are? Imagine the long-lasting effects this will have on children who are seeing this on the news. The same with the more recent attacks on our Asian population.

These cultural traumas we're living through, have altered our sense of security and will have the trickle-down effect for generations to come.

## Individual Trauma

Like the cultural, individual traumas are life changing no matter what age the trauma happens.

As children, it's those experiences that speed up childhood and dilute innocence. Things like growing up in extreme poverty where there's insecurity of basic needs like food and shelter. Or growing up in a dangerous neighborhood where unhealthy patterns are passed down just in order to survive.

Growing up with an alcoholic parent and all the trauma that brings over and over again, on so many deep, deep levels for everyone involved.

Growing up with a war veteran with PTSD, whose behavior may be unbalanced, and frightening to a child that doesn't understand, so the child grows up with fears or anxieties that they wouldn't otherwise have.

Then there's the even deeper s**t that happens within the family. You know the stuff that's not talked about, even when some family members know about it…Abuse.

Childhood abuse that causes *a cycle* of abuse and anxiety, whether it be emotional abuse where there is no parent-child attachment or verbal, physical or the unthinkable sexual abuse.

BTW, it doesn't always mean *doing* something. It can be just as traumatic if there's a blind eye turned towards the abuse. Like a mother that turned a blind eye to the abuse her husband was doing to their child. Unfortunately it happens all the time. It could be that *her* dad was an abusive alcoholic and *her* mom did nothing to stop the abuse. See the trickle-down effect? A parent or grandparent who didn't heal from their own trauma may find it difficult to give emotional support to someone *else* suffering their own trauma. The emotional detachment cycle trickles down.

The generational trauma happens when those experiences aren't talked about. When a child experiences abuse and doesn't get the chance to heal from it, the shame and abuse still haunts them as they grow older, leaving unresolved issues and fears that are passed down.

Spirit, the therapist on OWN says, "The impact is not something we're always consciously aware of. If they were physical wounds, we would see them and respond, but because they're emotional we can't see the wounds and the trauma can keep building until they manifest themselves in other ways."

They may try to numb the memory with alcohol or drugs which adds a whole next level layer of trauma, or become an abuser themselves. I'm sure you've heard the term "When the abused becomes the abuser?" That's GT.

Fact is, you can't deal with how you show up as an adult if you can't heal the trauma you experienced as a child. It impacts the way you love yourself and others, and the way you parent.

Trauma based responses carried over from childhood cause the pattern to continue; emotional detachment originally from protecting yourself continues as emotional detachment for your children. Control issues because you didn't have control when you were younger and someone took advantage of that… or a lifetime of limiting beliefs from constant verbal abuse…"You're a loser just like your father. You'll never do anything worthwhile."

Basically, hurt people…*hurt people*, and the trauma trickles down the genealogy tree.

Is any of this hitting home?

## Break The Cycle

Well, your life as it is today may be built on your past, but it doesn't have to be controlled by it. You have the right to break the chain. You don't have to continue to be a victim. Stop the trickle-down effect of abuse, abandonment issues, neglect, and addiction for yourself and those after you.

"Well that's the way I was raised" doesn't have to be how your children are raised. Things don't have to be the way "they've always been." Who decided that? Not you. Break that s**t up.

Take responsibility for creating change and break free from the unhealthy chains of generational beliefs and behaviors.

## It Ran In My Family...Until It Ran Into Me
The Pattern can stop with you.

A friend of mine has so much generational trauma that she wrote a book about it. Actually, I should say books! It's a trilogy. Yes, it took 3 books to go through her baggage. That's a lot to unpack but writing about it was a way of releasing it and letting it go. She's doing everything in her power to break *all* those chains for her children.

I understand it's scary. You've suppressed the feelings for so long that you don't want them to come up to the surface to have to deal. It seems easier to go numb than it is to sit in the feels. But when you put new trauma on top of old trauma it just keeps building on top of itself and settles in, weighing you down.

If you don't deal, nothing will ever change, and it will continue to impact your quality of life and the relationships you're in and those after you. So, don't push it back down. Have the courage to release it. Let it go for you and the generations to follow. You have the control and you don't need anyone's permission!

## How To Start Healing
Remember I said awareness is the first step in making a change? Start being aware. See the patterns; domestic violence, abuse, detachment, etc. Connect the dots between behaviors and choices from generational

experiences to your life today. Heal the childhood wounds that hold you back from giving love 100% or receiving love 100%.

Forgiveness is a necessary step to move forward. For your own peace of mind and to begin the healing process, try to understand that it was a cycle. In some cases, those that hurt you, carried their own generational trauma without knowing how to heal. It doesn't excuse it one bit, but it might explain it which will help in the healing process.

Don't wait for them to understand that though. Many people don't realize their behaviors are wrong, and never will, because it's what they learned growing up. Even if it's abnormal societal behavior, its normal to them. Make sense? Some people are *never* going to change, so, you have to take the control. You have the right to decide whether you want to keep the dysfunctional people in your life or let them go so it doesn't continue.

## Break the Chains that Bind

Not gonna lie…untangling yourself from GT can be a long process, but awareness, even if uncomfortable is the key to starting to break that pattern, especially one as secretive and complicated as this.

Here are 5 suggested steps from the website www.courage2connect.com to start the untangling.

- **The first step is seeing the patterns;** some are more obvious than others, like domestic violence, abuse, anxiety, and anger issues.

- **Second step is building awareness around what triggers you to step into these established patterns.** Is it yelling, disrespect, feeling devalued, physical aggression or watching people bully others?

- Once you're aware of your triggers, **the third step is becoming aware of how you react to the triggers.** Do you shut down, become angry, become violent, hit or yell?

- **Fourth Step is learning to put roadblocks in those patterns.** Yes, roadblocks. I know that this whole book is about removing roadblocks, but this is the one time we want to put some up. Set up a trigger word or phrase that helps you recognize when you're going down a pattern. Set up a network to be held accountable.

- **Fifth step is to give yourself grace.** These are patterns that have been ingrained for a long time. It doesn't heal overnight or over a week. It takes time.

This is just the start of what I hope will be a journey to awareness for those that are victims of generational trauma. Having said that, don't let yourself stay a victim…become the victor instead. To do that I recommend finding professional help. This is A.LOT. Real s**t. The brain doesn't always remember the traumas, but they're held in your body and soul, creating heavy, invisible baggage to be carrying around. To have the best chance at truly breaking the cycle once and for all, you need support to work through it and change the beliefs and patterns that the inherited trauma can leave.

It can be organized support groups, a recall therapist or preferably a professional therapist who specializes in PTSD. Therapy can help release you from the generational chain even if the people that were involved in creating it are no longer here.

## Whoever it is…talk to someone. It's not showing weakness. It shows strength. More strength than any of the generations before you had.

As some anonymous internet wisdom says… "When they tell you it runs in the family, you tell them this is where it runs the f**k out!"

So be the one! Be aware you need change, release your anger, find your voice, and show up differently in your life…for you, those you love and the generations to follow. It's never too late.

# HABITS; THE GOOD, THE BAD, & THE UGLY

*"It seems, in fact, as though the second half of a man's life is made up of nothing but the habits he has accumulated during the first half."*

Fyodor Dostoevsky

Google told me that Brad Pitt reportedly doesn't like bathing, so he'll go weeks without doing it, using baby wipes in between. Jessica Simpson doesn't brush her teeth every day, wiping her teeth with a cloth instead. And Kesha used to drink her own urine. I'm sorry. What?

Yours may not be as nasty as those, but we all have them. Some good, some bad, and some downright ugly. I'm talking habits; those small conscious decisions and actions you make every day that affect the quality of your life, and often the lives of your loved ones.

Think about it, your life today is a result of your habits. How in shape or overweight are you? How successful or unsuccessful are you? How financially stable? All are a result of your habits.

Made you think, didn't it?

### THE GOOD
The good habits lead us to being happier, healthier and wealthier. You know the ones; exercising, eating right, saving instead of frivolous spending. We could all use more of these. Duh!

### THE BAD
Ever been out at a dinner party and someone comically confesses their bad habit of say…always running late? And someone else joins in with theirs and suddenly, bad habits become the topic of conversation? That's because we *all* have bad habits and try to ease our embarrassment by making fun of them; the fact that we eat too much, shop too much or…are always running late. It's a form of the "Haha put down" we discussed in Chapter Seventeen. From snacking at midnight to procrastination, bad habits are a daily battle for most of us.

### THE UGLY
And then there's the ugly; the ones that aren't talked about at the dinner party but are discussed behind closed doors, if at all. Nothing to laugh about here. Those are the ones fought in a minute by minute battle and often take a dark turn and develop into addiction.

## Change Your Habits, Change Your Life
How are these habits formed? Well, our environment and the people we hang around…our tribe, can be part of the problem. But it's mostly all those little decisions that add up and the choices we make for better or for worse. So, to change your life you have to change your habits.

> **EVERYTHING IS A CHOICE AWAY, INCLUDING THE CHOICE TO CHANGE.**

Hanging on to bad and ugly habits weighs you down and gets in the way of living your best life. Continuing the bad and ugly habits, knowing they're blocking you and yet doing nothing to change them is getting in your way and killing your self-esteem. Wouldn't you talk to a friend you care about if you saw their bad habits blocking them from a better life? Well then, do it for you. Change for real this time. Don't just talk about it.

Everything is a choice away, including the choice to change. So why don't we change? Because whatever your thing is, whether it's bad or ugly, those habits have been a part of your life for so long they've become comfortable, even if they make your life *un*-comfortable. Get it?

There's an old proverb that says, "Bad habits are like a comfortable bed, easy to get into, but hard to get out of." Truth! Our fear of change and going out of our comfort zone is so strong that we continue the destructive behavior even though we know in some cases, as in some of the bad and ugly ones…it can literally kill us. We let ourselves become victim to it.

Sounds a bit crazy when you read it though, right? I mean anyone that has lived any kind of life knows you'll go through *more* discomfort if you continue to sabotage yourself with those habits. It's a vicious cycle.

## Disbelief And Denial

Another common reason for not changing a habit is we don't believe we have a problem, whether its disbelief or denial.

### Disbelief

You can't believe you have the problem a bad habit has caused, and when you come back to reality, you feel it's too late to change. "Whose body *is* this? When did *this* happen? Well, it's too late now. I'll never be able to lose the weight." Sound familiar? Well, as you now know…it's never too late to change.

### Denial

Don't let your bad habit become an addiction by denying it. If you find yourself spending all your time denying your bad habit to yourself and others; "I don't have a drinking problem" …it's an ugly one my friend and you need to do something about it.

## The Magic Bullet

Whatever it is, we all consciously want to break bad habits which is why New Year's resolutions are a thing. We try to change but get lazy and stuck in our comfort zones, that comfortable bed of bad habits, so those well intended resolutions usually don't see February. And another year goes by with us still stuck in the same bad habits feeling defeated. You've lived it, I've lived it, we've all lived it.

Because of that, people spend time and money, and buy from TV infomercials or Facebook ads at 2am trying to find the pill or magic bullet that will finally help them stop their bad habit or will be a shortcut to better habits. Anyone remember the "Thigh Master," or the "Shake Weight" that I may or may not have in my garage right now? Just sayin.

The crazy thing is…**You and your power to choose are the key.** And **Daily Discipline is the magic bullet** we've all been looking for. Something we've had all along and is free. What?

Yep. You're literally a choice away from changing your life. All you need to do to get your control back is...

> Choose to drop the bad habit that's weighing you down
>
> Have the chutzpah to stick to that choice
>
> Create the new good habit with daily discipline.

Boom! I know it's not as sexy as a TV infomercial product seems at 2am, but it is the magic bullet. It's that simple and yet that f*ing hard. Discipline is hard or we wouldn't all have a problem with it, but if you just take it one day at a time and make it a positive habit, it gets easier each day. I promise.

Here are a few examples of celebrities I read about that used their power of choice to change the habits weighing them down, and daily discipline to be successful.

Jennifer Aniston was a chain smoker but quit smoking in 2012. The daily discipline of yoga is what helped her kick that bad habit.

Adele was a self-proclaimed drunk. She chose to kick her ugly habit because hangovers were beginning to affect her money maker, her voice. She stopped drinking and is now living clean and healthy. Her voice is clearly fine now and the recent weight loss is a.ma.zing!

And we all know Oprah struggled with her weight for decades until Weight Watchers the second time around. The daily discipline and accountability were key in kicking her bad habits.

I'm no celebrity, but I can attest that daily discipline works in getting rid of bad habits and helping to develop the good ones. I recently went from looking like a "Before" picture in a weight loss ad, to 40 pounds lost so far and still counting.

I *chose to* change my lifestyle habits to more positive ones instead of the easy 2am miraculous diet pill purchase. I've lived long enough and made enough of those purchases in the past to know they don't work. Good old-fashioned daily discipline does. Concentrated daily discipline combined with my daily declarations and super suggestions, I went from destructive habits weighing me down, to building the good habits protecting and nourishing me.

Not gonna lie, this won't be easy. You'll step into the un-comfort zone temporarily. I did, but I made it out and it's no longer a struggle.

You have to love yourself more than the bad habits and deal with a little temporary discomfort to take back your personal power. You're worth it.

## Change It Is A Comin'

So, after "choosing to" change or get rid of a habit, the daily discipline is up to you. Here are some things that have helped others stay consistent and be successful.

- **Make a written commitment to yourself—a Habit Contract.** Decide on something as a reward for yourself for reaching a certain point in your new habit and write it down. Pick something that you wouldn't ordinarily get for yourself so it's extra special. For instance, a spa day for sticking to your new exercise plan for a month. Put it where you'll see it and it will keep you motivated. Rewards give you the emotional reward which is one of the top secrets to building long lasting healthy habits.

- **Don't forget "The Why"… you want to change.** This is a powerful one. Write down your reason for wanting to change and keep it posted where you can see it because it will get you through the times when you're tempted to quit.

- **Make it a "Choose to" not a "Have to".** This mind shift changes your subconscious thought process. Remember to be the boss of your attitude. When you realize you always have a choice, that you're the only one who's the boss of you and you "choose to" do it, you take charge and make it happen. This is the #1 thing for me being successful in changing my eating habits. Its crazy how simple and effective it is. 40 pounds lost so far and still counting…all because I decided to "choose to" eat healthier instead of saying to myself I "Have to" eat healthier and lose weight. Words are powerful!

- **Get motivation from whatever inspires you and keep it close by.** Your motivation may be as simple as a picture of your loved one that you're inspired to make the change for, or make a vision board. Whatever keeps you motivated, keep it nearby.

- **Get rid of anyone not on board with your change.** The toxic people in your life, like "junk food friends" or "drinking buddies" who enable you in your bad habits and try to keep you down with them are not your friends and are definitely baggage needing dumped.

- **Get someone to hold you accountable.** This is why *Weight Watchers* and *Alcoholics Anonymous* and others like them have been successful for so long. You're held accountable and it makes all the difference in your success.

- **Celebrate your wins and reward yourself.** When your goal has become a habit, give yourself the incentive you put on your habit contact and then start a new one!

## Handle Your Business

There are some bad and ugly habits that will be too daunting to handle alone and you'll need help from others. That's Ok. We all need help sometimes. Now is your time. The important thing is to choose to take it on now. Handle your business!

If you've had a lifelong battle with a certain habit, I recommend you talk to a professional to help you work through why you have this bad or ugly habit in the first place.

And reach out to the well-established organizations listed for help so you can get rid of it once and for all! Here's a list of some with a proven record of helping people and those they love, get through the bad and ugly habits.

- Alcoholics Anonymous… https://www.aa.org/
- For family and friends of alcoholics go to… https://al-anon.org/
- Gamblers Anonymous… http://www.gamblersanonymous.org/ga/
- For family and friends of Gamblers go to… https://gam-anon.org/
- Narconon; Drug Addiction Rehabilitation… https://www.narconon.org/
- Overeaters Anonymous… https://oa.org/
- Weight Watchers… https://www.weightwatchers.com/us/
- Sexual Addiction… https://saa-recovery.org/
- For family and friends affected go to… https://sanon.org/
- Domestic Abuse…National Domestic Violence Hotline… https://www.thehotline.org/
- For an interesting online radio station dedicated to recovery music go to… http://www.12stepradio.com/

- And you can reach out to the Substance Abuse and Mental Health Services Administration which is a part of the U. S. Department of Health and Human Services… https://www.samhsa.gov/

There's a quote by Maria Fontaine that says, "Don't let your habits become your prison." Exactly!

Get to the bottom of it once and for all, however you need to do it, so it doesn't continue to rear its ugly head and you can be rid of it for good. Nothing is impossible. You can do it. I know you can. When you get through to the other side, you and those in your world will be glad you did. 100%!

**Now is your time! It's never too late!**

## CHAPTER 21

# TURNING POINTS, DECISIONS AND A LIFE FULL OF SOMEDAY'S

*"One change leaves the way open for the introduction of others."*

Niccolo Machiavelli

I read in *Oprah* magazine that artist Andy Warhol was a sickly child and spent weeks at a time resting in his bed. His mother Julia moved his bed closer to the kitchen so she could keep an eye on him. Every day for lunch, she served him…wait for it…a piping hot bowl of Campbells soup, which became the subject of one of his most famous iconic painting series.

And that artist Frida Kahlo, now considered one of the greatest artists of our time, had a bus accident when she was younger, and while healing at home, passed the time away painting. Her mother rigged a mirror above her head and Frida discovered the love of self-portraits which she is now known for around the world.

I learned in the documentary, "D Wade; Life Unexpected," that when NBA player D Wade was a child sitting on the front porch steps with his sister one day, police officers came up the porch steps, put a gun in the back of little Dwayne's head and told him to take them to his mom, a known drug addict, who was inside the house.

After that experience, his older sister brought him on the bus cross town to their dad's house. She left him there as he was playing basketball with his brothers, and never came back to pick him up, to give him a better chance at a good life. As he got older, his dad built a basketball hoop at the house so the boys wouldn't have to leave the safety of the house to play. He played with them and never treated them any differently than if he had playing with adult men. That made the boys better players. Eventually his dad noticed that Dwayne started to show more talent than his brothers. The rest is history, with several obvious turning points that changed Dwayne's life.

## What Are Turning Points?

Turning points are the game changers in our lives. The times when something happens, causing a major shift that has you turning away from one path towards another, shaping and defining you along the way.

> MORE OFTEN, IT'S THE SMALLER EVERYDAY DECISIONS THAT SHAPE YOUR LIFE.

We experience many turning points in our lives. Some are a conscious choice, like marriage or a career change…or choosing to stop a bad or ugly habit as we just discussed in the last chapter. And then there are times when the *circumstances* we're in create the turning points that are life changing, like Andy, Frida and D Wade and we're not aware of it until later in life.

## Decisions

People tend to get hung up on the big decisions of life, but more often, it's the smaller everyday decisions that are usually made without thinking that shape your life and end up being more important.

Every day of your life you're faced with thousands of decisions and choices. Many times, we choose out of habit because we're so busy just trying to get through our day, that we don't give them much thought. But think about how some of those decisions can create turning points in our lives unintentionally, whether for better or worse. Choosing a healthy salad or a Bic Mac and fries everyday for lunch, could lead to a health turning point in the long run. Get it?

As a fun, trivial example here's Actor Richard Dreyfuss' turning point story. He was a working but relatively unknown actor when George Lucas suggested him to Steven Spielberg for the part of "Hooper" in the now classic 1979 thriller movie, "Jaws." Richard turned the role down *twice*. Then he saw the final cut of another movie he was in and saw how horrible he was in it. Out of sheer panic thinking no one would hire him after seeing that performance, he immediately called Spielberg and accepted that role in "Jaws" to assure he would have another job. Great Decision. "Jaws" ended up winning three academy awards, has people of a certain age still afraid to go in the water, and made Richard Dreyfus a bona fide movie star for decades. He made several little decisions that created an unexpected turning point in his life and career. Do you get the idea of how the little decisions in your life add up to a turning point?

One of the easiest ways to understand the importance of the little decisions is to think about the turning points in *your* life. Were they really the result of clear-cut decisions where you knew exactly what the outcome would lead to? Or were your turning points the result of a lot of *little* decisions that were made with hardly any or no thought of the consequences of your choices?

## A Choice Away

**You are always a choice away from changing your life…**choosing a new path. It's exciting if you think about it as the power you have every single day to make a decision that influences your life in a positive way.

You've already consciously chosen twice. A conscious turning point was choosing to buy this book. Yay you! And back in Chapter Thirteen, I said you were at a turning point; that you have a choice between staying as you are or having the courage to continue and change. You made a choice to keep growing. Great choice. You get the idea. One choice can change your world and create a turning point.

## Whitney

I've talked about not letting others dim your light, as Whitney did. Fact is we can also *dim our own light* with the choices we make. Sadly, I use Whitney again to emphasize my point.

I saw a tribute to Whitney Houston with some of her performances through the years. As I watched the compilation of several decades worth of performances, it was fascinating and yet painful to see through time elapse technology, the progression of changes in Whitney at the various stages of her life and career, **and the affects her life choices had on her**.

The young 19-year-old having just been discovered with raw talent and beauty. A few years later, a bit more polished as her star was beginning to rise, but still a young girl with that beaming smile. Fast forward through some good years when she became a full-grown International star and had the world at her feet.

Fast forward through some drama years… drugs, Bobby…then a surprise appearance at an awards show for her mentor Clive Davis, after having been out of the spotlight for a while dealing with her personal demons. Still beautiful, and her voice was still *that* voice, but she appeared tense, scared even…beaten down. And during the performance she no longer had that beaming smile. Instead it was a furrowed brow. Nor did she have the alluring confidence, she actually had her eyes closed through almost the whole performance as if to give herself courage just to get through it. Her light had dimmed dramatically.

She disappeared from the spotlight again, so fast forward many more years of drama…more drugs, more Bobby…after the Oprah interview where she "told all." Older, still beautiful but her voice now showing the signs of her decades of bad choices and self-abuse. She was making a comeback, Oprah crying as she sang the perfect comeback song, "I didn't know my own strength."

She was humbled and vulnerable but showing just a tease of that former confidence…ready to be the former Whitney again. Everyone was rooting for her to succeed. And then months later…we of course all know the tragic end to her story.

As I watched the show, I found myself crying. She was so blessed with her beauty, talent and a successful career and she threw it all away. Why? Her choices. I realize there was a lot more behind those choices that I'll never know, but still. What a shame. It's such a sad story of a wasted life all because of a bunch of little decisions that became bigger choices that became several turning points in her life until those choices ended it. She was always a choice away from saving herself, but she made other choices and *lived the life* of those choices…until she didn't.

Do you have a Whitney in your life, or are you maybe…?

## Procrastination…A Life Full Of Someday's

Have you ever seen someone with a clear opportunity for change in front of them, paralyzed by fear and indecision, or afraid to "rock the boat" of the relationship they're in? So, they instead choose to stay stuck, deciding to change "Someday." A life full of somedays is an extreme case of procrastination and can lead to such a small, small world. Ben Franklin said that the word "Someday" is equivalent to failure. Ouch! Procrastination kills goals, motivation, energy and self-esteem, and in some like Whitney, lives.

Think about it, when you put things off that you're avoiding whether it be an unopened bill, a trip to the doctor, or deciding to get rid of an ugly habit, it doesn't go away from your mind. It gnaws at you daily, making you feel even worse about yourself which can lead to more bad decisions and choices as you try to numb it and ignore it.

If you put off making a decision you're avoiding by even one more day, you've chosen to stay where you are like Whitney did. She had endless possibilities to make better decisions and get out of the smallness she got herself into but didn't. I'll bet she chose many times to make the change and quit her ugly habits "someday."

Those "somedays" often keep us from a bigger life. Procrastinating on not only life changing decisions, but decisions that could broaden and expand your mind and world. "I'll see Europe Someday" or "I'll do that drive cross country I've always wanted to do Someday." "I'll take that art class Someday."

## Well you can someday yourself right out of a life...literally.

Our current world has placed us in the land of "someday's" due to the Pandemic. You just never know. Life is more uncertain now than ever.

This is why I'm a *"why not?"* I don't have any regrets or a life of somedays! I have a Do it Now attitude!

## Do It Now!

We've talked about habits, and to change your life...you have to change your habits. That can be done by ***choosing to*** Do it Now!

A Do it Now attitude is one of the key habits of successful people. Don't waste your energy holding on to whatever you're delaying doing. It's draining holding off on calling the debt collector, or going to the doctor, or whatever your thing is. Free yourself up and Do it Now. Whether it's paying a bill, taking the opportunity to take that cross-country trip or finally seeing the doctor. You'll be amazed at how much more energy you have and how many more adventures, if you just Do it Now! And regarding the doctor...the reason I'm still here and now cancer free is by not delaying going to the doctor, therefore catching my cancer early enough to treat it successfully. So, if you've been putting that one off, Do it Now, not "Someday," or you may not have a someday.

## Combine your new Do it Now attitude with a "Why Not?" attitude...and watch out world, here you come!

Let me leave you with this from a man who was a "Why Not?" and lived his life as a dramatic example of someone with a Do it Now Attitude... our friend that you read about earlier, the adventurer John Goddard.

He wrote an exciting harrowing tale about his experience kayaking down the Nile. In it, he told of the fact that some tribes in Africa believe that when they go to sleep at night, they experience death, which is overcome each dawn as long as their souls remain in their bodies. As a consequence of this belief, they live a day-to-day existence, enjoying each day of their lives as if they had seen the dawn for the last time. Therefore, they don't waste any time in brooding over the troubles of the past, or the doubts, worries and fears of the future. They live for now...the present. What a great way to embrace life.

John already lived his life with that philosophy, but after he almost died on that kayaking trip, it became an even stronger conviction. In his book, he pronounced this Sanskrit poem as his favorite;

### *"Look to This Day"*

*"Look to this day, for it is Life, the very life of life;*
*In it's brief course lie all the verities and realities of our existence,*
*The bliss of growth,*
*The glory of action,*
*The splendor of beauty,*
*For yesterday is already a dream, and tomorrow is but a vision;*
*But today well–lived makes every yesterday a dream of happiness,*
*And every tomorrow a vision of hope.*
*Look well, therefore to this day.*
*Such is the salutation of the dream.*

Don't live a life of "Somedays." Look to this day, make the right little decisions, choose to live today well with a Do it Now attitude and your best life is yours.

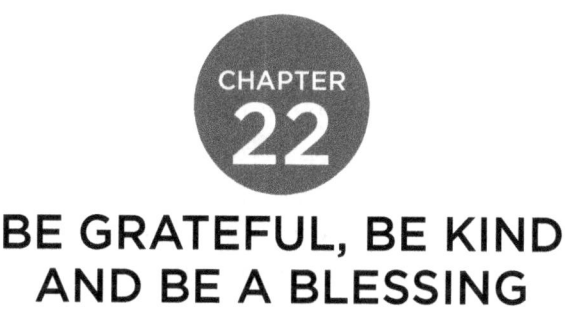

# BE GRATEFUL, BE KIND AND BE A BLESSING

*"Let gratitude be the pillow
upon which you kneel to say your nightly prayers."*

Maya Angelou

I'd like to leave you with three last thoughts, or suggestions really, to fit into your new Best Life.

 ## Be Grateful

Take the time to protect, appreciate and nourish the relationships of the people in your life that encourage you, support you and want the best for you. Those people that uplift you and that you're grateful for.

Let the people in your life know they are appreciated and valued. It's easy to get so wrapped up in ourselves that we take them for granted. So, make a list of the people who are important to you; your life partner, your children, your family, friends or employees. Put some thought into it.

Whoever it is, send a short note expressing your appreciation. Not only for the things they've done, but for who they are and what they mean to you. Even if you think they know, tell them anyway. Think how much it would mean to *you* to get a letter of appreciation from someone in your world.

BTW, I'm talking old school personal handwritten note or card if possible, sent via snail mail. Everyone's inbox is inundated with impersonal emails which just aren't the same, DM's don't quite have the personal touch, and definitely don't text your way out of showing your appreciation. No one sends handwritten notes anymore so it'll mean much more. Can you even remember the last time you got one in the mail?

For some, this is a hard ask because writing may not be your thing. I understand that, just write from the heart and "speak" your truth. Start with the people closest to you. That'll be a bit easier to get your flow going. You can also send flowers to someone special randomly. It's such a pleasant surprise when it's random and unexpected and will be remembered even more.

Point is, make someone's day, and make it something you do on a regular basis. The little time it takes to make it happen is nothing compared to the joy you'll bring to someone's day. Spread kindness. We all need it more than ever now.

And for yourself, I'd keep a Gratitude Journal to remind yourself of all that you have and the new changes in your life that you're grateful for. It helps keep you positive and focused, and attracting more to be grateful for.

## ③ Be Kind

Mother Theresa said to "Spread love everywhere you go. Let no one ever come to you without leaving happier." Yeah…do that! Being kind is doing that and living the Golden Rule. Anyone remember the Golden Rule? **"Do unto others as you would have them do unto you."**

The simplicity of that resonated with me early in life, so I've always tried to live my life that way. I'm not saying I'm a saint, by any stretch of the imagination or that I never do wrong, but I do make a conscious effort every day to do the right thing, treat others well, help someone in need and show the special people in my life my appreciation for what they contribute to my life.

That's the easy part. You also have to be kind to *yourself*, which has been the hard one for many of you in the past. But that was then…this is now. You've learned enough in this program to realize being kind to yourself is just as important.

## ③ Be A Blessing

And last but absolutely not least, be a blessing. Another example of living the Golden Rule.

My parents instilled in me a mentality of giving back. I don't remember it being talked about specifically, but I learned by their example. From my early teens into my forties I volunteered my time to help others.

I cherish those times, because there's never been anything more rewarding to me than those experiences of making someone else's life better. My available time has been more limited since then, but I still donate financially. It's important to me to support organizations that do the right thing for people or animals that have been wronged, or people not given the opportunities in life that I have been blessed with. That's why I've committed to donating a percentage of every sale

I make to various charities throughout the year, starting with this book and online course.

To truly be whole, to be complete, each of us needs to be a blessing to other people. Do some volunteering of your time to an organization close to your heart. Or do something for someone in your family or community. See if your parents need something done around the house. No matter how tired my wonderful big brother was from his demanding career, he gave up his Saturday's every weekend to take my mom out to breakfast, get her a mani/pedi and then do together whatever errands she needed done. She looked forward to that time together with him every week. He was a true blessing to her, and still is to me and all who know him.

How about helping mentor our youth? There's a shortage of "Big Brothers," so my best friend decided to help a single mom friend of ours with her teenage son. She mentors him as much as possible and helps him with school and homework. English is the second language for this family, so my friend helps communicate with teachers, even having one on one meetings with the teachers on his mother's behalf. She does that and so much more, making a difference in his life and so many others. She is a blessing to all who know her and is the epitome of kindness and living the Golden Rule! That's what I'm talking about. Can you say the same?

So with that in mind…Be Grateful, Be Kind, and Be a Blessing to your self and others.

Congratulations. You've made the *very* intentional shift and your world is gloriously changing. Embrace it! Your future is full of possibilities. Your future's so bright…you gotta wear shades!

And always remember…

## You Don't Need Anyone's Permission to Live your Best Life!

# CHAPTER 23

# WHAT'S NEXT?

*"The beautiful thing about learning is that no one can take it away from you."*

B. B. King

You did it! Woo Hoo!!! You made it through! Congrat's on building your foundational power! Doesn't it feel great to take your power back and be in control of your life again? You should be very proud of yourself!

So, what do you do next?

First let me tell you what you don't do. What you *don't* do is think that since you completed the book, you're done. Don't put this on the shelf, forgetting all about it and abandoning the work you've done to this point. As writer Martha Beck says, "hold tight to your breakthrough, because once your eyes have been opened, trust me when I say that it will not feel good to close them again."

## You Are A Warrior

These past few weeks you've worked hard to choose your path and clear any roadblocks on it. You've been a Bad Ass! So, keep at it. Continue using the powerful lifelong principles you've learned to keep your path clear. **Once you've unpacked those bags, you need to make a conscious effort to not pick them up again.**

And continue to pay attention to *You!* Don't fall back into living someone else's life. You've worked too hard and know too much now to let yourself fall backwards.

Consistently integrate these powerful principles into your life. Live it with every choice you make. Choose to keep doing your Daily Declarations, your Grown Up Time Out and your Super Suggestion. Re-read the book, or go through it with your family.

## But Wait...There's More

- **Online Course**

    Better yet, take my interactive 7 module online course based on the book. It's next level and you're ready for it. I actually guide you through the lessons because I talk through the presentations, giving more explanation and sharing some of my personal stories.

    The game changer though is the downloadable action worksheets designed to help reinforce all the principles you're learning and apply them in real time to your life. With the purchase of the course, you also get membership in our private online community… "No Permission Society"…a community of others doing the positive work to live their best life, and where I join in and communicate regularly.

# WHAT'S NEXT

Did I mention you get two special mystery boxes of cool YDNAP swag mailed out to you when you sign up, and at the end, as a congratulations for completing the course?

Scan the QR code to learn more, or sign up using your book buyers code BB21 to receive your exclusive 50% discount.

- **Life Coaching VIP Packages**

  If you would like individual guidance, we have Life Coaching packages available with special VIP rates for my readers. Scan the QR code to learn more.

- **FB & IG Communities**

  Please join us online @youdontneedanyonespermission.

- **Stay Connected**

  No matter what… please stay involved with us. Be the first to hear when new books and courses are available, and I'm always grateful hearing your stories and feedback…especially testimonials of how this helped you to your best life. Sign up for our mailing list at www.youdontneedanyonespermission.com to stay connected.

So, with all that said…you're really at a beginning. A beginning of living your life intentionally. Your Best Life! Thanks for letting me be a part of it.

Donna

www.ingramcontent.com/pod-product-compliance
Lightning Source LLC
Chambersburg PA
CBHW071732080526
44588CB00013B/1995